A History of

Best wishes
to Carol

Pamela Southworth 28·07·2007.

A
HISTORY
OF
SWINESHEAD

by

Pamela A. Southworth

In association with
The History of Boston Project

19 96

Richard Kay
80 Sleaford Road • Boston • Lincolnshire PE21 8EU

© Pamela A. Southworth 1996
ISBN 0 902662 17 1 (cased edition)
First published by Richard Kay Publications December 1996
Reprinted with minor typographical corrections March 1997
0 902663 07 4 (paperback edition) April 1997

Typeset by the publisher initially in Microsoft Word™ and PageMaker™ on an AppleMacintosh™ and output in camera-ready copy which was then manipulated via Rank Xerox Media Server. Printed electronically, in Bookman typeface for the body of the text, at 420 dpi resolution at 135 pages per minute on a Rank Xerox DocuTech™ 135 Laser Production Publishing System by:

Foxe Laser
Enterprise Road • Mablethorpe • Lincolnshire. LN12 1NB

CONTENTS

Page No.

ILLUSTRATIONS

Sponsors and Subscribers

The author, the publisher, and the History of Boston Project are most grateful to all those persons and institutions who, by their sponsorship and subscription, have greatly facilitated the production and publication of this book.

Sponsors

Dr and Mrs Richard Allday— Boston
Dora Box— Little Gaddesden
C. M. Davies— Swineshead
Mr and Mrs Fred Gilding— Swineshead
Anne M. Gosling— Boston
Ann Grundy— Boston
Sheila and Jim Hopkins— Boston
Lincolnshire Libraries
Norah Shaw— Boston

Subscribers

Isabel Bailey— Boston
Mrs A. M. E. Baker— Pinchbeck
Rev M. A. Barsley— Swineshead
Mrs Marion E. Bavin— Stickford
(Mrs) K. J. Beecham— Frampton
Boston High School
Irene Bowens— Boston
F. Bramwell— Boston
Mr and Mrs W.J.Brunt
— Wyberton
Mr and Mrs J. H. Burrell
— Swineshead
Kathleen Burrell— Swineshead
Pamela Clark— Westharbour,
Auckland N.Z.

R. Ernest Coley— Boston
Dr J. T. Cope— Swineshead
T. S. Crosby— Rickmansworth
Mrs J. Cuthbert— South
Normanton
R. W. Dales— Mablethorpe
Mr and Mrs B. Dawson
— Swineshead
R. Drury— Lincoln
Mr and Mrs A. Dudgeon
— Burnley
Ted Eaglen— Boston
J. Emmitt— Swineshead
Dr and Mrs M. J. Fairman
— Boston

SUBSCRIBERS (CONTINUED)

P. and J. Flynn— Boston
Richard H. Foster— Swineshead
Jean Francis— Frampton
Grant Fulgham— Camarillo,
               California
Mr and Mrs John Gillett— Boston
Hilary Healey— Bicker
The Heritage Trust
          of Lincolnshire
Pamela and David Hopkins
  — Redwood City, California
J. and B. Hughes— Boston
Garth Isaac— Boston
Mr and Mrs D. James
        — Chesterfield
Mr and Mrs A. Johnson
        — Swineshead
Jane Keightley— Boston
Frank King— Wigtoft
Mrs J. A. Lavelle— Settle
W. J. McDonald— Swineshead
Derrick Meeds— Boston
J. C. Morgan— Islington
Dr and Mrs Mowbray
     — Farnborough, (Hants.)
Mrs E. Presgrave— Boston

Edward John Russell— Worthing
R. Sales— Swineshead
Mr and Mrs B. Scotney— Boston
Chris Scotney (Car Sales)
        — Swineshead
Mrs M. Scotney— Swineshead
M. E. Sharp— Frampton
Gloria Sheen— Richmond Hill,
              Ontario
Mr T. D. Slade— Kirton Holme
Collingwood Smith— Swineshead
Mrs Janet Smith— Southgate
Mr J. Southworth— Blackburn
W. J. Southworth— Ipswich
Mr and Mrs E. R. Sylvester
        — Boston
Tim Sylvester— Boston
G. Neil Webster— Swineshead
Nancy Wilcox— Swineshead
George H. Wilkinson— Boston
G. Wilson— Swineshead
Mr and Mrs N. Woodcock
        — Wyberton
Eric Woods— Kirton End
David Wright— Swineshead

Glossary of Terms Used in the Text

Advowson: The right of presentation to a benefice by a bishop or layman. Lay patronage dated from the 8th century when laymen began to build churches on their land.

Bailiff: 'General Manager'.

Berewick: Demesne land detached from the lord's hall.

Bloxham: Village near Banbury, Oxfordshire.

Bolingbroke: The Honour of Bolingbroke was a part of the Duchy of Lancaster. When Henry of Bolingbroke, son of John of Gaunt, became Henry IV in 1399, the Duchy of Lancaster became vested in the sovereign. [See also Lancaster.]

Bordar: Cottager.

Bovate (or oxgang): An eighth of a carucate.

Burgh: An Anglo-Saxon fortified dwelling or town.

Capacities: Papal licences to acquire benefices.

Carucate: As much land as one oxen team could plough in a year. Between 100 and 160 acres. This varied in different parts of the country.

Conversi: Lay brethren.

Court Baron: A meeting of freehold tenants, held by the lord of the manor.

Court Leet: A court of record held by the lord of the manor.

Demesne: Land held by the lord.

Divine service: Spiritual tenure with the obligation to say masses.

Domesday: This was a record of the possessions of each land owner and the tax due from individuals.

Fee: Word derived from 'fief' meaning free heritable tenement

Frankalmoigne: Spiritual tenure requiring the giving of free alms.

Frankpledge: Twice yearly inspection by the sheriff of the system of tithings.

Free socage: A residual tenure of land, neither service, spiritual or military.

Gelt/geld: Money, usually a tax.

Glebeland: Land attached to the parish church.

Grange: Farm attached to an abbey, usually outlying and manned by lay brothers who farmed the land. They were, in effect, small religious houses. The man in charge was called a granger. By the 16th century most granges were in lay hands.

Hayward: Supervisor of haymaking.

Heckler: One who combed out flax or hemp.

Hides: An Anglo-Saxon unit of land of a size considered sufficient to support a peasant and his household. Thought to have been 120 acres (approx) in the eastern shires where it became known as 'ploughland'. In Wessex it was as little as 40 acres. Hides were the basic unit of assessment for taxation and military service.

Hidage: An assessment of tax and military service due from each shire based on the number of hides in the shire. The eighth century document 'Tribal Hidage' assesses the taxable capacity of Mercia.

Honour: The sum of lands held by a tenant-in-chief. The honour originated as a centre of military command in Norman times but within 100 years it often encompassed estates scattered throughout the kingdom. The honorial court was held at the 'head' of the honour, which was usually its largest castle.

Hundred: Similar to a wapentake, a term used in other parts of the country. A division of a county originally supposed to contain 100 families (Chambers Twentieth Century Dictionary). Dates from Anglo-Saxon times to the nineteenth century and was used south of the River Tees. Varies in size from area to area. It may have originated from groupings of 100 hides. Hundred Courts met every 4 weeks. They had jurisdiction in cases relating to local issues and also apportioned taxes. The term survives today in the Chiltern Hundreds.

Inquisition/post mortem: An inquiry held on the death of a tenant in chief to confirm the date of death, to ascertain what lands the deceased held 'in capite', and to identify the heir.

Knight's Fee: A tenement held by knight service.

Knight Service: Military service in return for a grant of land.

Lancaster: The Duchy of Lancaster had land in all parts of the country, including the honours of Lancaster, Tickhill, Bolingbroke and Knaresborough. The first Earl of Lancaster was Edmund Plantagenet, son of Henry III. Edward III made Lancashire a county palatine in 1351 in favour of Henry, first Duke of Lancaster. This meant that the Duke had similar powers to the king within the county of Lancashire, in particular the control of the law courts and appointment of judges. When Henry of Bolingbroke, Duke of Lancaster, became King Henry IV in 1399, the Duchy of Lancaster became vested in the sovereign, although remaining separated from the crown. After 1399, therefore, if a man held land of the Honour of Bolingbroke, he actually held it of the king.

Outdoor Relief: Money and/or food and clothing given to the poor to maintain themselves in their own homes.

Patronage: The right of control of appointment to an office or priviledge to an ecclesiastical benefice.

Pinder: Keeper of the pound.

Reeve: Foreman.

Right of Common: The right to pasture sheep & cattle on the common land belonging to the parish. This could also include the right to gather firewood and cut turves.

Sac: The possession of power and privilege, granted to an individual to hear and determine disputes, levy fines etc.

Scutage: Money paid in lieu of military service. This was common in the 12th and 13th centuries.

Selion: Strips of land sometimes known as a rig or ridge. Most villages had two open fields which were divided into selions .

Serf: A peasant who held no land. He had to work the lord's land and was not allowed to leave the manor.

Serjeanty: Services rendered to the king for tenure of land.

Sixhills: Small village near Market Rasen in Lincolnshire.

Soke: This was a territory in which the sac and other privileges were exercised.

Sokelands: See Berewick.

Sokeman: Tenant who held land by performing certain husbandry services for the lord.

Steward: Chief officer.

Stover: Winter food for cattle.

Tewing: To haul or tow.

Tenter: One who tends, attendant, shepherd, cowherd.

Thegn: An Anglo-Saxon lord, the king's man.

Tod: An old wool weight, about 28lbs.

Vill: Estate centre.

Villein: A peasant bound to his lord by legal ties. He usually had some land of his own to plough. He also had to work for the lord of the manor for 2 or 3 days a week.

Wapentake: An administrative subdivision of the northern and central English Shires in which Danish influence predominated. The word is derived from the Old Norse for weapons and take; taking and grasping weapons was probably a Viking way of signifying assent at a meeting. The wapentakes were the units of tax assessment and each wapentake was responsible for maintaining law and order in its own jurisdiction.

INTRODUCTION AND ACKNOWLEDGEMENTS

Although I was born in Boston I lived in Swineshead for twenty years, seven years in High Street and thirteen on Tarry Hill. My three children were born and raised there, and all attended the village school. One of their favourite places for a pic-nic was the Manwarings, and they spent many hours cycling around the village or walking the dog down the back lanes.

During the course of tracing my family history a few years ago, I discovered that there was once a workhouse on Tarry Hill. Having lived not far from the site of this workhouse I was intrigued to know more. I am only an amateur historian, but have researched the history of Swineshead to the best of my ability, and recorded all that I could of its story.

During the course of the two years spent researching and writing this book, I have spoken to many local people, and I would like to thank them for providing me with material from their own scrapbooks, photograph albums, and family records, and also for their suggestions of further sources. I would also like to thank them for the hospitality they have shown by inviting me into their homes.

I would like to thank in particular Mr and Mrs John Burrell, Miss Kathleen Burrell, Mrs Joyce Cuthbert, Mrs Winifred Crunkhorn, Mr and Mrs Barry Dawson, Mrs Jenny Emmett, Mr and Mrs Richard Holland, Mrs June Holland, Mr Tony Johnson, Mr Colin Luesby, Miss Ann Macroric, Mrs Pam McDonald, Mrs Beryl Mason, Dr and Mrs Mowbray, Mr Philip Reynolds, Mrs Doreen Rowley, Mr Brian Simmons, Mr Colin Smith, Miss Mary Smith, Mr and Mrs Maurice Scotney, Mr Christopher Scotney, Mr and Mrs Barry Woods, and Mr and Mrs Jack Weekley.

I would also like to thank the staff of both Boston and Lincoln Libraries, and the staff of the Lincolnshire Archives for their help and guidance, and their patience.

Lastly I would like to thank my dear husband for his help. He has transcribed documents, checked my typescript and been a constant source of encouragement. I dedicate this book to him.

CHAPTER ONE

THE BEGINNINGS

WHERE COULD YOU FIND an Italian duke and a Norman count; a ruined abbey and a medieval church; a pious Abbot and a dying King; ancient crosses and a moated castle; Romans, Saxons and Danes; several manors; a market and a fair; and in more recent times four windmills, a brewery and fourteen public houses? Swineshead, at one time had all these and more.

But to begin at the beginning . . .

It is unlikely that the area of Swineshead was ever inhabited by prehistoric man as, in early times, the entire region was under water in a large bay. About 125 AD changes began to take place as the sea receded. Low lying islands appeared in the Wash and a large area of land around present day Swineshead emerged from the waters. It was about then that the first signs of human habitation appeared, in the shape of Roman salt pans.

There were two methods of producing salt from sea water. Firstly natural depressions or 'pans' were filled with sea water which evaporated naturally leaving behind the salt. Secondly, there was the open pan evaporation process where brine in shallow pans was heated from below. It is difficult to say with any certainty which method was used in the Swineshead area but the latter process is the most likely as this was a procedure introduced to this country by the Romans. Archaeological evidence has identified salterns at Coney Hill, North Lodge, Low Grounds and Broad Ings. (The Domesday book records eighteen salt pans in the area).

There is other evidence of settlement at this time, involving trade as well as manufacture, in the shape of pottery made in what is now the County of Warwickshire, and other pottery from Gaul (Roman France). Both Samian and grey ware shards have been found locally.

1.

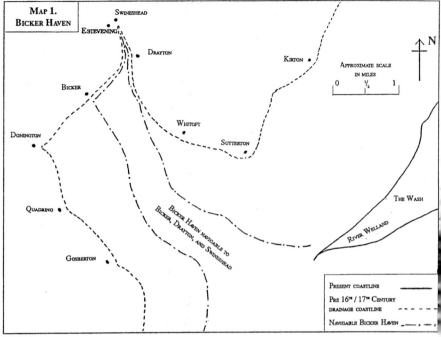

1. A sketch map of Bicker Haven and the changing coastline

Sometime in the later part of the fourth century the sea level began to rise again. This may have been a factor causing the Romans to leave the area, though other reasons may have been increased harassment from bands of Scandinavian raiders, or demands from their home country. The higher sea level probably made the area uninhabitable until about the mid seventh century when the sea receded once more, and Saxons began to repopulate the region.

It seems likely that Drayton and Estevening were the two settlements that came into being first. Drayton developed near the mouth of the tidal creek known as the Swin, with Estevening a little further inland. Map 1 shows the relative locations of these two settlements, as well as the probable coastline and the navigable Bicker Haven, before the early drainage attempts of the sixteenth and seventeenth centuries.

It has been suggested that the name Drayton derives from the word 'draught' or 'dray' (draw) and means a place where boats were drawn up. If that derivation is correct then it could suggest that boats were hauled up a creek (perhaps the Haff) too narrow for the use of oars, or simply drawn up on a beach. The Haff ran from the haven towards Baythorpe.

Estevening possibly derives from the word 'estover' meaning a tenant's right to gather wood from another's estate for repairs or the making of implements.

Swineshead is said to have been named after the River Swin on which it developed. This poses the question 'How did the river Swin get its name?' Local tradition has it that the Swin began at Northend and ran into the sea at Drayton, which would have made it a remarkably short river.

The old Scandinavian word 'svein' and the Old English word 'swin' both mean a tidal creek or inlet. 'Heda' is an Anglo-Saxon name-ending, meaning dock or landing place. It is fairly certain that this is the derivation of the name Swineshead—a landing place on a tidal creek. The detail on Map 1 supports the view that the Swin was a short tidal creek rather than a river.

Probably the earliest record of Swineshead is in the Anglo-Saxon Chronicles in the year 675 AD:

> 'Wulfhere, son of Penda, and Aescwine son of Centus fought at Biedanheafde. In the same year Wulfere passed away and Aethelred received the Kingdom.
>
> In his time, he sent bishop Wilfred to Rome, to him who then was pope—he was called Agatho—and told him by letter and word how his brothers, Penda and Wulfhere, and the abbot Saxulf, had built the monastery at Peterborough, and that they had freed it of all service to bishops and kings: he asked him that he affirm it with his deed and blessing'

The Pope replied to Aethelred confirming this in 680 AD. The King (Aethelred) called a council meeting at Hatfield and had the

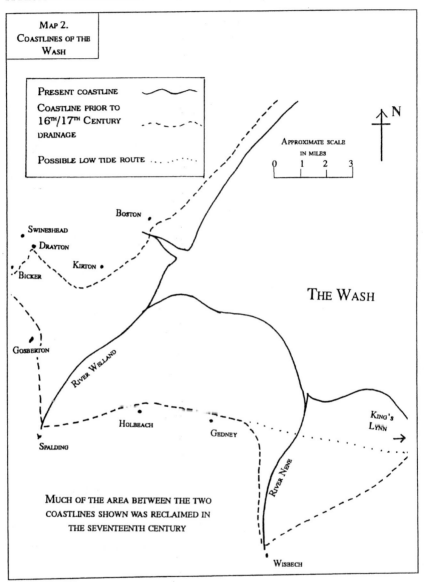

MAP 2.
COASTLINES OF THE
WASH

PRESENT COASTLINE

COASTLINE PRIOR TO
16TH/17TH CENTURY
DRAINAGE

POSSIBLE LOW TIDE ROUTE

N

APPROXIMATE SCALE
IN MILES

0   1   2   3

BOSTON

SWINESHEAD

DRAYTON

KIRTON

BICKER

THE WASH

GOSBERTON

RIVER WELLAND

HOLBEACH

GEDNEY

KING'S
LYNN

SPALDING

RIVER NENE

MUCH OF THE AREA BETWEEN THE TWO
COASTLINES SHOWN WAS RECLAIMED IN
THE SEVENTEENTH CENTURY

WISBECH

2. Coastlines of the Wash

Pope's deed read to his council. At this meeting the King said:

'. . . I give St Peter today into his monastery at Peterborough these lands and all that belongs thereto, that is Breedon-on-the-hill, Rippingale, Cedenac, Swineshead, Heanbyrig, Lodeshac, Shifnal, Cotesford, Stratford, Wattlesborough, the Lizard, Aethelhuniglond and Bardney.'

The deed confirming this gift was signed by:

'Theodorus, Archbishop of Canterbury; Wilfrid, Archbishop of York; Saxulf, who was first abbot and was now bishop; Osthryth, Aethelred's queen; Adrianus—a legate; Putta, bishop of Rochester; Waldhere, bishop of London; Cuthbald, abbot'

There is also another mention of Swineshead, in the Anglo-Saxon Chronicles, for the year 779:

'In the days of King Offa there was an abbot in Peterborough called Beonna. This same Beonna, through the counsel of all the monks of the monastery, let to ealdorman Cuthbricht ten tenant farms in Swineshead with pasture and with meadow, and all that belongs thereto . . .'

It was almost one hundred years later, in 865/6, that the Danes invaded East Anglia, and according to local tradition established a camp near Swineshead. This 'Viking encampment' of tradition is reputedly sited at the 'Manwarings'. The Manwarings is a circular raised mound 1.8 metres above the level of the surrounding land, encircled by two moats. The inner moat is 15-17 metres wide and the outer moat is 7-10 metres wide. The mound is 47 metres in diameter and covers 1740 square metres. It is claimed to be unique in being the only circular moated site in the Holland area of Lincolnshire, and stands in the fields at Baythorpe, not far from the site of the Abbey.

Danish fortifications were usually D shaped and built by a river. The river was used as the straight side of the D, and a semi-circular moat was then dug to surround the camp. This could have been the case in Swineshead, as the tidal creek known as the Haff flowed up to the Abbey and possibly to the Manwarings.

However not all Danish encampments were D shaped. Some circular sites have been found in other parts of the country, namely Warham Camp in Norfolk, which has been proved to have originated in the Iron Age, but may have been remodelled by the Danes; Ringmere, also in Norfolk, a circular enclosure 30 metres in diameter; and Howbury, in Bedfordshire, which is a circular enclosure 40 metres in diameter with ramparts 3 metres high, surrounded by a water filled ditch. The present circular form of the Manwarings does not preclude it from being a Danish site. It could have been D shaped and subsequently changed, or it could have been circular originally.

The possiblity of the Manwarings being of Danish origin cannot be lightly dismissed, although there is no supporting arch-aeological evidence. The present land contours suggest that it was the site of a Norman motte and bailey castle. It may be that as the Viking's encampment at Warham was built on an earlier Iron Age fort, so a Norman motte and bailey castle was built on the site of an earlier Danish camp.

The story of the Manwarings may have been first set down in about 1813 in W Marrat's book *Sketches Historical and Descriptive in the county of Lincoln* where he states unequivocally ' . . . there was formerly a Danish Encampment called the Man-war-rings. It consists of a round hill on which buildings have stood'. It was probably this same publication which was the origin of the legend that a tunnel ran from the Manwarings to the Abbey, for Marrat goes on to say 'a sub-terraneous passage is said to have led from this hill to the abbey'. Swineshead inhabitants will be aware that the nature of the land and the high water table throw doubts on this being possible, and again there is no evidence for a tunnel (although aerial photographs show that there may have been a roadway between the two).

Both these stories have gained credence through the years by constant repetition, both verbally and in newspaper articles and other publications. One such article earlier this century, written under the pseudonym 'Benedict', claimed even earlier origins for the mound, saying it 'was probably cast up in prehistoric times by the then inhabitants of the district'. The writer then claims that it was an Anglo-Saxon administrative centre and the place where the 'Moot Court' was held. Again there is no evidence to support these claims, although each hundred (or wapentake) had at that time an open air meeting place, where cases of theft or violence and other matters were heard, and it was usually a circular mound 25 metres across surrounded by a ditch.

Despite a lack of hard evidence in the way of records or artefacts to prove the existence of any settlement, as no archaeological digging has taken place at the Manwarings, it would have been most unlikely if there had not been a Viking encampment somewhere in the area. The Danes invaded all along the east coast including the Wash and other East Anglian shores in 865/6 AD. It was in about 868 AD that these conquerors fired the monasteries of Peterborough, Crowland and Ely. It is almost certain, therefore, that part of this force at least would have penetrated the Wash as far as Drayton and Bicker, and near these natural harbours would have set up a camp or camps to serve and protect the same.

It has been suggested that there was a camp in the neighbourhood, under the control of Hubba, a Dane, (after whom Hubbert's Bridge is reputedly named) and it may well be that this is the origin of the legend which over the passing years has become linked with the Manwarings. (The name Manwarings is probably a corruption of Manor Ings, meaning, quite simply, the meadows of the manor). Whether or not the Manwarings was ever a Danish encampment it is almost certain that the existing mound was raised circa 1080/90 by a Norman lord, following the Conquest.

After invading England, in 1066, William the Conqueror divided up the country between his barons. Land around Swineshead was given to his nephew Count Alan of Brittany. Count Alan received the land of the Saxon, Edwin, eldest son of Algar, Earl of Mercia, who had his chief residence at Kirton. Count Alan, also known as

Alan Rufus, was the founder of the Honour of Richmond, and according to one writer, Pishey Thompson, Drayton was his principal seat.

The Manwarings was probably the site of a castle of Count Alan, occupied by his overseers in the area, where he would stay when visiting his lands here. It is doubtful if it was his principal seat. This motte and bailey castle (or defended manor house) was probably built circa 1080-1100. It has a central circular mound (motte), surrounded by two deep ditches, formerly serving as inner and outer moats. The original building/s would probably have been built of wood and surrounded by a wooden palisade (bailey). Pieces of clay roof tiles and fragments of medieval pottery have been found in the area, but no traces of any wooden construction have survived.

The castle would have had a relatively short life, because of the wooden structure which would decay. Before the year 1200, wooden castles began to be replaced by stone, but no foundations have been found to suggest that this castle was ever built of stone.

It has been suggested that the Manwarings was the site of the manor house of 'The Manor of the Moor'. The identity of this manor is unclear but surviving Court Rolls of the Manor of the Moor, where copyhold property tenancies are recorded, contain the entry, in 1641, 'Elizabeth Lockton (cottage etc from her father, William Lockton, esq, Lord of this Manor)'. The Manor of the Moor could be the Abbey Manor, or Drayton Manor, both of which were held by William Lockton, or even Baythorpe Manor. The manor house of the Abbey Manor was not sited at the Manwarings, but still exists today, substantially altered, on its original site in the Abbey grounds.

The next record of consequence concerning the area around Swineshead is the Domesday Book (1086), a survey ordered by William the Conqueror, of property and land holdings throughout the country. Swineshead itself is not referred to in the Domesday Book, but both Drayton and Stenning (Estevening) do appear:

'The Land of Earl Alan, Threo Wapentake.

SPECIAL NOTICE.

The REVIEW -- ADMISSION: FREE.

2nd. V. B. LINCOLN REGT.

A REVIEW

of the Boston and Gosberton Companies of the 2nd V. B Lincoln Regiment and the 3rd V. B., E. D. Royal Artillery Boston will take place at the

OLD DANISH ENCAMPMENT

SWINESHEAD,

By permission of Mr GEORGE SMITH.

On Monday July, 22nd. 1889.

A ZEREBA

will be erected and defended by the Artillery and the G Company, the C Company forming the attacking force.

AFTER THE SHAM FIGHT A

BATTALION DRILL AND MARCH PAST

WILL TAKE PLACE.

The G Company will assemble at the Market Place, Swineshead, at 6 p. m. in full dress Uniform; and headed by the Swineshead Band (kindly placed at the disposal of the Corps) will march to the Old Camp Ground when operations will be commenced at once.

A Supper will be given to the Volunteers, Donations respectfully solicited. Treasurer- Mr G. SMITH, Hon.-Secs- Mr R. THORPE. & J. G. SMITH

M. J. JOHNSON, PRINTER, SWINESHEAD,

3. A poster of 1889 advertising an event at the Manwarings.

9.

Manor. In Drayton (Draitone) Hundred, Greve had six bovates of land rateable to gelt: the land is six bovates. Toli the Earl's vassal, has now there one carucate in the demesne and four villeins and four bordars with one carucate, and ten acres of meadow and half a salt-works worth 8d yearly. The annual value in King Edward's time was 16s; it is the same now.

In the same Drayton, Wulfin the Bishop had one carucate of land rateable to gelt: the land is one carucate; and it belonged to St Benedict of Ramsey, according to the testimony of the jurors of the Wapentake but they say that they know not by what right (the Bishop) held the same. Earl Alan has now there two bordars, and eight acres of meadow land and one salt-works worth 16d yearly. The annual value in King Edward's time was 3s; it is now 2s.

The Land of Earl Alan.
Drayton Hundred.
Manor. In Drayton itself Ralph the Standard-bearer had eight carucates and two bovates of land rateable to gelt: the land is eight carucates. The land is soke in the vill itself. Earl Alan has now there six villeins, and six sokemen, and one bordar, who have five carucates. There are also four salt-works and a half worth 6s yearly and forty acres of meadow. In the time of King Edward the annual value of Drayton [Hundred] with all the appurtenances belonging there to, was 30l: it is now worth 70l; and it is tallaged at 20l.

Land of Count Alan, Bicker Hundred.
In Stenning Halfdan had three carucates of land taxable. Land for three ploughs. Geoffrey (of) Tournai the Count's man, has two ploughs.
Eight villagers who have half a plough. Six salt-houses, 8s. Meadow fifty acres.

10.

Value before 1066, 20s; now the same.

The Land of Colegrim.
Soke. In Drayton Wider had half a carucate of land rateable to gelt: the land is half a carucate. It is Soke of Drayton, the Manor of Earl Alan. Godric has there three bordars and two acres of meadow.

Land of St Guthlac's Abbey, Croyland, Berewick of this Manor.
In Drayton (Draitone) is one carucate of land rateable to gelt: the land is one carucate, (and although there are) five villeins there, they do not plough. there are also four salt-works worth 5s 4d yearly, and six acres of meadow land.

Land of Robert of Vessey.
In Stenning Aelfric had six bovates of land taxable. Land for six oxen.
Robert has: one villager; two salt-houses at 2s 8d; one fishery which pays 200 eels; meadow 18 acres.
Value before 1066 and now, 20s.'

From the two following entries in the Domesday Book, it seems there was a dispute over the ownership of certain land:

'The Land of Wido de Credun.
In Drayton Alestan had half a carucate of land rateable to gelt: the land is four bovates. This land was delivered to Wido for a Manor and he has there one villein and four bordars with half a carucate, and two acres of meadow. The annual value in King Edward's time was 5s; it is now 3s.

Claims in Kesteven.
Wido de Credun holds in Drayton four bovates and in Bicker Hundred ten bovates of the land of Adestan, which was Godramesune's. Earl Alan claims these

(lands) and Algar his vassal has pledged himself to the King's barons to prove by ordeal or battle that Adestan himself was never seized of these fourteen bovates in the time of King Edward. On the other side Wido's vassal, Alestan of Frampton, has given his pledge to convince them that he was seized thereof with sac and soke; and that Wido has been seized thereof from the time of Ralph the Standard-bearer, until now, and that he now holds the same.'

[Wido de Credun, also known as Guy de Croun, came over with William the Conqueror. His seat was at Freiston.]

Apart from farming, salt production also took place in both Drayton and Stenning.

The number of saltpans in the locality as stated in the Domesday Book entries above was as follows:

Drayton	4 saltpans rendering	5s. 4d
	1/2 Saltpan rendering	. 8d
	1 saltpan rendering	.16d
	4 1/2 saltpans rendering	6s. 0d
Stenning	6 saltpans rendering	8s. 0d
	2 saltpans rendering	2s. 8d

Half a salt pan indicates one shared by two people.

It will be noticed from the extracts above that Drayton, at the time of Domesday, was itself a Hundred (or Wapentake), but Stenning came under the Hundred of Bicker.

It is not easy to interpret the total land in these entries, but it seems that in Drayton there were 12 carucates of land, 68 acres of which was meadow. Whilst one carucate equals eight bovates, these measures were variable and it is impossible to interpret them exactly. A carucate could be between 100 and 160 acres. At the lower estimate Drayton manor would have been about 1200 acres. As Drayton was on the coast, then this land would have been to the north of Drayton, perhaps embracing the present day settlements of Swineshead, Swineshead Bridge, Brothertoft,

Hubbert's Bridge and Kirton Holme.

Note that in Drayton manor there were thirty six individuals (14 bordars, 16 villeins, and 6 sokemen) employed by the lord. If one assumes that a quarter of these were either unmarried men or elderly without family, then one can roughly estimate that there were about 27 families or households in the area at that time.

In the early 1100's the manor of Drayton came into the possession of Robert Gresley, who shortly afterwards founded Swineshead Abbey.

4. A carved figure of a boar's head on the parish church.
[Or perhaps a 'swines' head', but not the derivation of the village's name.]

Footnote: During World War II the War Department dug an underground bunker in the mound known as The Manwarings, to use as an ammunition dump. Nothing of archaeological value was recorded.

CHAPTER TWO

THE ABBEY

THE FOUNDATION OF ST MARY'S ABBEY at Swineshead dates from February 1135. It was founded by Robert de Greslei who endowed it with 240 acres of demesne land. The abbey was initially supplied with eleven monks from Furness Abbey, its 'mother house'. At that time it was part of the Order of Savigny. However Savigny merged with Citeaux in September of 1147 and the monks of Swineshead Abbey became members of the Cistercian Order. Swineshead Abbey pre-dated the other Cistercian houses of Kirkstead (1139), Louth Park (1139) and Revesby (1142).

The Cistercian Order originated in 1098 at Citeaux, in Burgundy, France. It was a very disciplined order and the monks lived a simple life, farming in remote areas. They chose to be self-contained and self-sufficient. The Fens suited them admirably. They had a very frugal lifestyle and rejected all comforts, managing without cloaks, hoods and shirts, and wearing only a white habit. This led to them being known as 'white monks' to distinguish them from the Benedictines who wore black habits and were known as 'black monks'. The Cistercians renounced all possessions, and incomes of the church, such as advowsons, altar and burial dues, and tithes. Even their crucifixes were made of painted wood and not precious metals.

A typical day in the life of the monks would have begun around 2am. They would then spend time in prayer until about 7am, when the following hour was devoted to reading. They were then allowed to return to their dormitory to wash themselves and change into their day shoes, after which they returned to the choir for Mass.

From 10.00 am until noon they did manual work, after which came more prayers, and dinner was served at 2.00 pm. The majority of the monks would have had no breakfast, the only people who did being the cook, the lay brothers and the young monks (novitiates), who were allowed some bread and wine. In winter there was only one meal a day, but in summer both dinner and supper were served. After dinner there was more reading from 3.00 pm to 5.00 pm, followed by Vespers, after which the monks retired at 7.00 pm.

The food eaten at dinner would consist of bread and vegetables, with dishes made from fish, eggs, milk, cheese and flour. Honey was served as an occasional treat, but meat and lard were forbidden, except to the sick. The evening meal in summer would only be of bread, fruit and raw vegetables. A drink of water was allowed at bedtime. Beer was never drunk by the Cistercians, although the Benedictines had a daily allowance and they were also allowed to eat meat.

The Cistercians lived a much simpler life altogether than the Benedictines. They worked in silence wherever possible, only speaking when it was unavoidable, as in instructing the novices. The novices only entered the novitiate at the age of sixteen in a Cistercian house, whereas the Bendictines took children at a very early age and trained them in a special school.

The white monks introduced 'conversi' or lay brothers, who worked their farms, thus leaving the monks more time for prayer. These lay brothers were illiterate and were expected to remain so. They learnt their prayers by heart, the few that were necessary for them, and they spent much less time in prayer than the monks. They generally lived outside the abbey at a 'grange' or farm, which could be anywhere up to twenty miles from the abbey, depending on the spread of the abbey lands. The grange consisted of a collection of farm buildings with a dining area and dormitory, and a small oratory for prayers. Swineshead Abbey's Hardwick Grange, close by the abbey, exists today as a farm, though nothing remains of the original buildings. The Abbey also had a dairy farm, known as a 'vaccaria' at Toft, or Brothertoft as it is now known.

The abbot of the house was elected by the other monks. The abbot of the mother house (Furness in this case) would preside, after advising on the choice of a suitable monk for the post. The elected abbot then appointed all the other officials. These were the provost or prior, who was next in seniority to the abbot; the chaplains who were secretaries to the abbot; the cellarer, who controlled all the material resources of the abbey such as food and drink, and maintained the stocks of flour, and fish, and also looked after the bees; the kitchener, who prepared the food and drink; the gardener; the chamberlain, who was responsible for clothing the monks and supplying them with shoes; and the cantor who was in charge of the liturgical and literary choral service in the church.

Swineshead Abbey was built of stone which probably came from Barnack near Stamford, as did the stone for the later building of Swineshead church and also St Botolph's in Boston. It would have been brought via the Welland and Bicker Haven to reach the abbey by way of the Haff, a tidal inlet adjoining the Swin but running up towards the Abbey.

Most abbeys were well appointed with all the required amenities and Swineshead abbey would have been no exception. It would have had a bakehouse, a brewhouse, various workshops including a tannery where they would make their own shoes, and a group of farm buildings. There would be a large garden with a fish pond. One of the monks would be a cobbler, another a carpenter, a mason, a tailor and so on. The monks would also have a library, an infirmary for the sick, and there may have been a hostelry for travellers.

The Cistercian monks were possibly the first people to undertake drainage work locally, to increase the amount of land available for pasture. They raised sheep for meat and wool, and exported surplus wool to the continent. There is a record of them exporting to Italy in 1300

Swineshead Abbey owned a house and garden near to Boston, close to 'Boston ford' and the Abbot is reputed to have travelled there by barge on occasions via the original Hammond Beck which flowed to the north of Swineshead. This house would have been his residence whilst conducting business in the town.

Whilst the Cistercians originally set out to lead a simple life, as time went on they gradually acquired wealth and land. Between 1166 and 1179 Swineshead, along with Furness, was in trouble for 'owning villages, serfs and courts'. The Pope, Alexander III, wrote 'a strong letter of remonstrance' to them both, but this seemed to have little effect.

King Henry the Second's confirmation charter enumerated the different donations which formed the endowment of Swineshead abbey. This showed that the monks owned land in Cotgrave, Nottinghamshire, amounting to half the town and manor; land in Casterton; the income from the mills of Burtoft, Sudwell, Manchester, Caldecot and Casterton; and also 240 acres of demesne land in Swineshead, which included Hardwick Grange. This charter also exempted the monks from all tolls, taxes, fines, and 'all secular exaction which belonged to the king'.

The abbey's numerous benefactors included both King Henry the Second and his son Richard the First. Among other benefactors were the founders Robert de Gresley and his son Albert; Stephen Earl of Brittany; Robert de Archis; Alan de Croun; Gilbert de Ghent; Simon, Earl of Montfort; Robert Russell; William de Vilers; and Henry de Longchamp. Henry de Longchamp died in 1274 and was buried at the Abbey.

In his will, dated 8th January 1397, Sir John de la Warre, Knight, left 500 marks to the the abbey of Swineshead. But it was not only the noble families who donated money to the abbey. Occasionally local trades people and their families left money for prayers to be said for them after their death. Elizabeth Rede, wife of a Boston merchant John Rede, left in her will dated 1485, £10 to the 'Abbey of Swyneshede', 'so that they make my husband and me broder and sister in their religion'.

In 1291, according to the Taxation of Pope Nicholas the Fourth, the ecclesiastical revenues of the abbey were as follows:

	£.	s.	d
Dioc. Linc. in decanat. Rotel temp			
abbatis de Swyneshed	3	6	8
In decanatibus de Gosecote	17	19	0
Frameland	28	3	4
Akele	53	4	4
Sparkenhon	11	6	4
Gudlakston	7	16	5
	121	16	1

NB: In decanatibus de = from the deanery of.

By 1534 the abbey's income was £167.15s.3d. That same year the bells and lead were valued at £274.3s.

At the dissolution of the monasteries, the Crown Bailliffs declared the abbey's income to be £184.17s.8d, and as this was below £200, the abbey fell under the First Act of Suppression in 1536, when the smaller monasteries were dissolved. At this time the abbey had ten monks and John Haddingham was the abbot. At the dissolution he received a pension of £24 per annum and the monks were paid 20s each, with capacities.

An early abbot of Swineshead was Gilbert de Hoyland (Holland) who was living before 1200, and was a disciple of St Bernard of Citeaux. Gilbert achieved fame by continuing the writings of St Bernard, composing forty eight sermons in the same style. Gilbert was highly thought of by his contempories, being 'a most excellent pastor' and teaching the monks 'with diligent perseverence, not only the letters, but also the excellent morality which he had himself so carefully and laboriously cultivated'.

Among other abbots were Robert Denton, living some time before 1203; William, who was abbot in 1203 and 1209, and who was mentioned in the Lincolnshire Assize Rolls as having some kind of dispute with Alan of Dowdyke over land in Swineshead; Robert, who circa 1226 granted Godfrey, the son of Robert of Surfleet, a tract of land in Gosberton; Lambert living in 1298; and John, who was elected in 1308 and was recorded again in 1338. The abbot in 1401 was William, and John Hadyngham was the abbot from 1529 to the Dissolution in 1536. There must have been others but there seems to be no record of their names.

The seal of the Abbot of Swineshead has been described as 'a pointed oval fourteenth century seal representing an abbot full length, in the right hand a pastoral staff, in left hand a book, with three monks on each side under a carved cinque-foiled arch or canopy crocketed. Above an embattled parapet in a niche with carved ogee arch having a flying buttress at each side, the Virgin, with crown, seated, the Child on the left knee. In the field 3 estoiles; in base, a boars head.'

The Abbot of Furness would visit occasionally to oversee the running of the abbey and dispense justice.

19.

In 1401 a certain Ralf de Byker was accused of 'having laid violent hands' upon a former abbot, and of stealing goods belonging to the monastery. He was found guilty and sentenced to imprisonment, but the day after being sentenced he escaped. Some time later he entered the abbey of St Mary Graces in London as a novice. When it was discovered that he was formerly from Swineshead Abbey he had to get a dispensation from the Pope absolving him, and releasing him from his responsibilities to the abbot of Swineshead. There were other incidents of this nature recorded in 1329 when three monks left the abbey taking with them some of its goods; and another monk had been absolved in 1314 for a similar misdemeanor.

The best known story of Swineshead Abbey is that concerning King John, who was supposedly fatally poisoned during his stay there in 1216, after having lost all his baggage in the Wash. It seems that only part of King John's baggage train was lost, having been caught by the incoming tide when crossing a ford near Wisbech over the now extinct Wellstream river. There is a traditional belief that the accident occurred near Sutton Bridge and it has been suggested that most of the items that were lost could have been recovered at low tide.

King John owned several crowns of state including a golden coronet with which he was crowned Duke of Normandy. He also owned a magnificent crown and other regal emblems which he received from the Emperor Henry VI in 1208. All these are reputed to have been among the treasures he lost in the Wash. This story could be supported by the fact that King John's son, Henry III, was crowned at Gloucester with a simple circlet of gold, rather than with a crown.

The following story of the death of King John, taken from a Manuscript Chronicle of England, is probably an early version:

> 'And in the same tyme, the Pope sente into England a legate, that men caled Swals, and he was prest cardinal of Rome for the mayntene King Johnes cause agens the barons of England, but the barons had a so much pte (poustie ie power) through Lewys, the kinges sonne of France, that king

Johne wist not wher to wend ne gone; and so hitt fell, that he would have gone to Suchold, and as he went the durward, he came to the abbey of Swineshead, and there he abode 2 days. And as he sate at meat, he askyd a monke of the house, how moche a lofe was worth, that was before hym sett at the table and the monk sayd that loffe was worth but one halfpenny. 'O' quod the kyng, 'this is a grette cheppe of brede: now' sayd the Kynge, 'and yff I may, such a loffe shall be worth xxd, or halfe a year be gone.' and when he had sayd the worde, moche he thought, and oft tymes sighed, and nome, and etc and sayde: 'By Gode, the worde, that I have spokyn shall be sothe.' The monk that stode before the kynge, was full sorry in his herte; and thought he himself wold suffer peteous deth; and thought yff he myght ordeyne therefore sum remedye. And anon the monke went unto hys abbot and was schryvgd of him, and told the abbott all that the kynge said and prayed his abbot to assayl him, for he wold gyffe the kynge such a wassayle, that all England shuld glad and joyful thereof. Tho wente the monke unto a gardene, and fonde a tode therein; and take hyr upp, and put hyr in a cuppe, and filled it with gode ale, and pryked hyr in every place, in the cuppe, till the venome came out in every place, and brought hitt before the kynge, and knelyd and sayd, 'Sir Wassayle; for never in your lyffe dranke ye offe suche a cuppe.' 'Begin, monke,' quod the kynge; and the monke drank a great draute, and toke the kynge the cuppe, and the kynge also dranke a grett draute and sett downe the cuppe. The monke anon wente to the Farmerey, and ther dyed anone, on whose soull Gode have mercye, Amen. And v monkes synge for his soull ispecially and shall while the abbey standeth. The kynge was anonfull evil at ese and commanded to remove the table, and askyd after the monke; and men told hym that he was ded, for his wombe (body) was broken in sondur. When the kynge heard thys tidyings he commanded for to trusse (bind); but all hitt was for naughte, for his bely began to swelle for the drinke that he dranke, that he dyed within 11 dayes the moro aftur Seynt Luke a daye.'

It is unlikely that this story is true, as King John is believed to have been ill before he reached Swineshead. Some claim that he

5. An old engraving illustrating one account of the poisoning of King John.

was suffering from a fever, perhaps caused as a result of his untimely soaking by the tide when he lost his baggage, although other versions of this episode claim that only the tail of John's retinue was caught by the tide, and the king was not personally involved.

Cornelius Brown in his *Annals of Newark on Trent* (1879) relates some other old legends on the subject of King John's death:

> 'Walter Hemingford (or rather Hemingburgh), who died in 1347, tells us that the King hearing the Abbot of Swineshead had a fair sister, a prioress in the neighbourhood, sent for her; that the abbot was uneasy about it, and the hospitaller of the monastery said to him, 'Do but absolve me, father, and pray for me, and I will rid the earth of this monster.'; that the abbot was scrupulous, because he was a king; that the hospitaller proceeded, nevertheless, and as he knew the king loved new pears, brought some that were all poisoned, except three that he had marked, and offered them to him; upon which the precious stones (in the king's rings) began to sweat. The king said to his host 'What is this you have brought me? Poison?.' 'Not poison,' said he 'but excellent fruit.' The king, by way of precaution, bade him eat one, which he did, taking one he had marked; then he bade him eat another and he did so; then a third, after which the king ate one himself, and died the same night.'

Another account given by John Fox from the 'Fructus temporum' agrees as to the manner of poisoning the king, but says it was on account of the language he had used to describe 'Lewis the Dauphin', who was highly thought of at Swineshead Abbey.

Matthew Paris, another early writer, suggests that 'grief and anxiety' were thought to have brought on the king's illness and had 'thrown him into a fever'. Paris suggests that the illness was aggravated by the drinking of too much rough cider made from local apples. This part of the country was celebrated for its pippins, called Kirton Pippins, which apparently made excellent cider.

Richard de Morins, author of *Annals of Dunstable*, who died in

1242, says, without any mention of poisoning, that the king died in the castle of Newark, 'in crastino Sancte Lucae', that is the day after the feast of St Luke, [ie the 18th October.] The *Annals of Morgan* which terminate in 1232, and the *Annals of Waverley* written about the same time, only say that the king died after three or four days illness at Newark.

A further suggestion of enmity towards King John arises from the following. In 1210 the king, being desperate for money, extracted large sums from all the Cistercian abbeys which, previously, had been exempt from such demands. This caused the abbeys great financial distress and some of them had to close as a result. These included the abbey of Meaux, and Fountains abbey. Both were closed for some time, their monks taking refuge at other Cistercian houses throughout the country, there being too many of them to be accommodated at any one house. It was not an uncommon sight in John's reign to see white monks begging in the streets. John's actions must certainly have made enemies within the ranks of the Cistercians.

It has been suggested that King John avoided staying overnight at Spalding Priory, as he knew he was unpopular there because of certain fines he had imposed on the landowners in that area. He was also involved in a lawsuit with Crowland Abbey.

King John arrived at Swineshead Abbey on 12th October 1216, and remained there for three days. When he left he was too ill to ride, and was carried on a litter to Newark. The party reached Newark on the 16th October where King John was treated by the Abbot of Croxton, who was known to be an able phyoician However it was too late and the King died on the 18th or 19th of October. It is recorded that his servants immediately robbed him of all his household goods.

At Newark, knowing he was dying, King John made a hasty will as follows:

> 'I, John, King of England, Lord of Ireland, Duke of Normandy and Aquitaine, Count of Anjou, being afflicted with a grievous sickness which, having not sufficient strength to bear, it behoveth me to provide for all mine by making my

will concerning my affairs. I commit the lawful administration and distribution of my will to the trust and direction of my faithful counsellors, without whose advice even when in health I would in no wise direct, but particularly at the present instant; and that what they shall honestly direct and order concerning my affairs may be lawful and binding, as well in making satisfaction to God and Holy Church for all indignities offered, damages sustained, and injuries brought upon it by any means; as in giving succour to the land of Jerusalem, in procuring aid to my sons for the purpose of seeking and maintaining their inheritance, and in remunerating those who have faithfully served us; in making distribution to the Poor, and to religious houses for the salvation of my soul. And I pray that he who shall give advice and assistance in fulfillling my Will may possess the grace and favour of God; but he who shall disturb its administration and order may incur the curse and indignation of almighty God, of the blessed Mary, and of all the Saints.

IMPRIMIS; therefore I will that my body shall be buried in the church of St Mary and Wulstan of Worcester. And I appoint as such administrators and distributors Lord G, by the grace of God titular Cardinal of the Church of St Martin, Legate of the holy church; Lord Peter, Bishop of Winchester; Lord Richard, Bishop of Chichester; Lord Sylvester, Bishop of Worcester; William Mareshall, Earl of Pembroke; Robert, Earl of West Chester; William, Earl Ferrars; W. Browne; Walter de Lacy; John de Monemut; Savery de Maleo; Faulk de Brent.'

Before leaving the story of King John, it is interesting to note that there was an ancient legend that, being aware of his sins, he was afraid he would be refused entry at the Gates of Heaven. He therefore insisted on being buried in a monk's habit. The story goes that he hoped to escape recognition by this ploy. Some credence was given to this legend when, in 1797, King John's tomb in Worcester Cathedral was opened and it was found that his skull was covered by the rotting remains of a monk's cowl.

King John was not the only king to have stayed at Swineshead Abbey. There is a record of a visit by Edward I in 1311, when he was entertained by Janin le Tregettur (John the Conjuror) in a private room at the abbey. King Edward may have had some attachment to the area, for he is recorded as visiting the fens in the winter of 1316: ' . . . that he might refresh his soul with the solace of many waters'

After the dissolution of the monasteries their estates were sold through the Court of Augmentation. The site of the ruined abbey at Swineshead was granted in 1552 to Edward Lord Clinton.

By 1607 the abbey lands had been acquired by Sir John Lockton, who built himself a house there, using the stones from the ruined abbey. Sir John Lockton was born in 1554, the son of John Lockton and his first wife Alice.

His father, John Lockton senior, who died in 1585, had originated in Sawston near Cambridge but was said to have been 'after of Swinsted, Co. Lincoln'. In his will John Locton senior requested that his body be buried in Swineshead Church, although he left 10s to 'Mr Harrison Vicar of Kirton for a sermon at my burial'. He left 40s to the churchwardens of Swineshead and £15 to the poor of the village. He also left 12d to 'the Mother Church of Lincoln'. His second wife Margaret was to 'enjoy the land I bought of Maister Hollans during her natural life; also the house at Downham in Norfolk which is hers.' His brother Philip Lockton, and his brother-in-law William Howson, were the supervisors of the will. His son Sir John, who was his chief beneficiary, received 'all my lands and hereditaments in England and all Annuities.'

Sir John Lockton had acquired, during his lifetime, the site of the old abbey, and at his death was also in possession of the properties of Drayton Hall and Orme Hall in Kirton.

There must have been a family connection with the Ormes of Kirton as their coat of arms, a heron between three escalops, was over the door of the abbey manor house. Sir John Lockton's own coat of arms was described as 'a chevron in bordure, crest a griffin's head holding a padlock'

Sir John Lockton did not live long to enjoy his newly built house as he died in 1610/11 and was buried on 17th January. In his

6. Sir John Lockton's family memorial in St Mary's church.

7. A stone effigy of a knight on the parish church.
Could this be a likeness of Sir John Lockton?

27.

will he requested that he be buried in the 'quire of Swineshead Church', where he used to sit, or 'as near to it as thought fit by my Executrix'. He left £6 13s 4d to the poor of Swineshead and Wigtoft, to be distributed by his wife, Dame Frances.

This was not the first time Swineshead had received benefits from the Lockton family. Robert Lockton, in 1593, had left 6s.8d. for repairs to Swineshead church, and 6d. each for 80 poor people. Philip Lockton, Sir John's uncle, whose will is dated 10th April 1599, left the poor of Swineshead £3 to be used by the Churchwardens for buying coal 'at the best and cheapest time of the year, to be resold to the Poor in Winter'.

Sir John Lockton married Frances, the daughter of William Howson of Wigtoft, and they had a large family, most of whom died in infancy or childhood. Their daughter Susan lived to become an adult but died in 1615. The following is an inventory of her goods taken after her death.

'An Inventory of all the goodes and chatells and moveables and immoveables of Susan Lockton late of Swineshead made the . . . . 4th day of May 1615.

It: In her purse and apparrell	20.00.00
It: One assignment of a pcell of a lease called by the name of Hardwicke Grange with the appurtenances belonging to the saide Grange sett over & assigned to her by Sir John Lockton her father for the termes of the said lease	120.00.00
It: Seaven kine & one hetter	10.00.00
It: syx yeareling bullocks	3.00.00
It: syx sheepe	1.16.00
the totall some is	154.16.00

Debtes oweing by the saide entestate to me John Lockton of Swineshead	5.10.00
To me Frances Lockton of the same	11.00.00
Debtes oweing to the saide intestate Thomas Hall of Swineshead	00.15.00
Debts deducted there remaineth	137.11.00

8th daie Mai 1615'

(The John Lockton mentioned in this inventory would probably be Susan's brother John, her father having died in 1610/11).

At his death Sir John had three sons still living, William, John and Francis. William the eldest son inherited the Abbey which passed down through his descendants. (See the family tree in the appendix).

Sir John's third son Francis married Ann Bradley of Louth, where he must have lived, as he and his family were buried there. Francis had seven children, one of whom, John, appears in the Royalist Composition Papers of 1646, where he is described as being 'seized of lands in Swineshead'.

Sir John's wife, Dame Francis Lockton, outlived him by another twenty years and died in Kings Lynn. The following is a shortened version of her will taken from 'Notes on the Visitation of Lincolnshire'.

'Dame Frances Lockton, Widow, of King's Linn, in the County of Norfolk, 25 Oct 1630. To be buried in Swineshead Church as near my husband the late Sir John Lockton Knight as may be. Poor of Swineshead £5 at my Funeral and Poor of Wigtoft 40s. To William Lockton Esq my eldest son £10 and 6 gilt spoons, four of which are marked W L. To my son John Lockton £100 and my best Chest in Drayton, my Furniture at Drayton Hall, and my bedding at Lynn. To John son of my 3rd son Francis, 2 dark Fillies. To Edward Lockton son to my son Francis, one spout pot. To Frances daughter to my said son Francis £100 at 21 or marriage. To my Maid a Riding Habit which was my daughter Susan's. To Thomas Watson and to Francis Hygge £5 each. To Elizabeth, Thomas, Robert, John and Mary, children to my son William 20s each at 21. To Frances Lockton daughter of said William Lockton £20 at 21. To my Nephew Roger Howson 1 little gilt Wine Bowl. To John Baker of Wigtoft and Margaret his Wife a Ring of the price of 10s each. To John Symonds 20s, and to his son Francis £5 at 21. To Robert Lockton 10s. To Thomas Ray and Walter Garnons 10s each. To my son Francis and his heirs all my lands and my Jewellery, Household Goods and Chattels. My Son Francis Lockton, sole Executor. Supervisors, my loving Brother Bradley Esq and Robert Osney Esq, 20s each.

Witnesses, Thomas Raye, Thomas Cronnell, John Booth, Walter Garnons.

Proved PCC (6, Seagar) 31 May 1634, by the executor.'

William Lockton, the eldest son of Sir John and Dame Frances, married Elizabeth Langton and they had three children. Elizabeth the first born died in infancy; their son John died aged thirteen; and a second daughter also called Elizabeth died unmarried at the age of thirty nine.

It would seem that William's wife Elizabeth predeceased him some time circa 1608/9. About six years later William re-married. The pedigree given at the visitation of 1634 gives his second wife as 'Audry daur of .... Reading 2 wife'. But in William's will dated 20th October 1657, he refers to 'Ann my wife'. This suggests that William had three wives, Elizabeth, Audrey and Ann.

Thomas, the eldest child of the second marriage and heir apparent, died some time between 1647 and 1657, predeceasing his father. The other children of this marriage were Rose, who married Thomas Dickenson; Mary; Robert who died in infancy; Frances, who married Henry Reston; a second Robert who died in infancy; a third Robert living in 1630; George who died in infancy, and John who married Frances Humphreys and eventually succeeded his father.

William and Elizabeth's second daughter Elizabeth, died in 1647 and was buried at Swineshead on 9th August. She died unmarried and left most of her estate to her sister Rose, after making the following bequests:

Item I give to Wm Lockton esq my father one warming pan.

It: I give unto Thomas Lockton gent my eldest brother all my sheep.

It: I give unto John Lockton my brother my grey mare & foals & a filly which was bred out of the said mare.

It: I give unto the said John Lockton my brother, my crimson coloured velvett petticoat with two gold laces and a gold fringe about it, and one gold ring with this posey in it, I like and love EP, and one great cabinet which was his mothers' and all things within it.

It: I give unto Frances Lockton my youngest sister, 12 pence.

It: I give unto my cousin William Lockton two gold rings.

It: I give unto Alice Tompson the daughter of Robert Tompson gent one green damask petticoat bound about with a silver galoone lace.

It: I give to my cousin William Balderston of Wigtoft £3.

It: I give to Ann Harne one silver gilt wine bolle [bowl] one brown cow with a white face which cow I bought off my brother Thomas Lockton,

It: I give more unto her one Holland handkerche and a pair of cuffs both set about with a tape lace, a Holland apron and my wascott wrought with black silk.

It: I give unto my servants 5s apeece.

It: I give unto Mabel Barnes 10s.

It: I give unto Robert Risbrooke 40s.

It: I give unto Alice Humbleton 10s.

It: to Widow Hamond 5s.

It: I give unto Ann the wife of Mr Lyndson(?) of Skerbecke Quarter my black -?- 2 year old -?-.

It: I will unto Rose Lockton my sister and to her heirs and assigns forever one tenement with appurtenances and half an acre of hemp land to the same tenement belonging being situate in the pish of Wigtoft, which I bought of the above named William Lockton which now in the tenure of William Carlton and William -?- and all other my goods and chattels ready money, plate, jewels, debts and household stuff not before bequeathed to Rose Lockton my sister whom I make my full and sole executrix'.

Dated 22nd July 1647.

There is also in existence an inventory of her goods.

The Inventorie of the goods Chettels & (Cattle?) of Mrs (ie Mistress) Elizabeth Lockton Deceased eldest daughter of Willm Lockton of Swineshead Abbey in the County of Lincoln made -?- or praised or written (by) Willm Balderston Robt Baguley & Willm Hudson the xxth day of January in the xxiijth yeare of the Raigne of our Sovraigne

Lord Charles, By the Grace of God of England, Scotland
ffrance & England Kinge Defender of the Faith etc anno dom
1647

	£	s.	d.
Imprimis her purse and Apparell	40.	0.	0.
Item one greate Trunke wth sevrall pieces of fine Linnen & silkes	20.	0.	0.
Item one little Trunke wth plate -?- silkes & fine Linnen	35.	0.	0.
Item one trusse Bedd two trundle Bedds foure featherBedds & other Beddinge & furniture	12.	0.	0.
Item Linnen fine & course	10.	0.	0.
Item Three Trunkes	0.	15.	0.
Item Two Chestes	0.	8.	0.
Item Two Cupbords	0.	14.	0.
Item Three Tables	1.	3.	4.
Item foure Chaires	1.	0.	0.
Item Two Stooles & a forme	0.	6.	8.
Item a paire of Virginalls	1.	0.	0.
Item Three little Boxes	0.	6.	0.
Item five Cushions	0.	12.	0.
Item pewter & Brasse	4.	6.	8.
Item an Iron Mill & a -?-	1.	0.	0.
Item five Irons Cobirons Andirons fire shovels Tongues & Spitts	3.	10.	0.
Item Wooden Vessell	2.	10.	0.
Item Two Warmering Panns	0.	10.	0.
Item Barrells & Beare stoole	1.	0.	0.
Item Wheeles & Reeles	0.	10.	0.
Item Eight Cowes, three Steares, three Quees, Three Steare Curlings & 4 Yearlinges Calves	50.	0.	0.
Item one horse, one Mare & Foale & a filly	10.	0.	0.
Item five sheepe	2.	10.	0.
Item swine	2.	0.	0.
Item Butter & Cheese	3.	0.	0.
Item Corne & Haye	3.	10.	0.
Item pullen & other things unseen & forgotten	1.	0.	0.
Debts			

32.

Item of Robt Thomson gent	10. 0. 0.
Item of William Lockton gent	16. 0. 0.
Sum Tot	234. 11.8.

Out of which is to be abated for Rent	11. 00. 0
Soe there Remaynes	223. 11. 8

Wm Balderston	Proved in April 1648
Robt Baguley (his mark)	Kirton in Holland'
Willm Hudson (his mark)	

(The question marks indicate words impossible to read or places where there was damage to the document).

From these documents it is possible to build up a picture of the house known as Swineshead Abbey, particularly from the will of Elizabeth's father, William. At this time the demesne lands of the abbey included two deer parks, the Great Deer Park and the Lesser Deer Park, the Plague Pits, the Monks' Fish Pond, the Butcher's Close, the Crow Park, and the Great Retting Pits.

According to Mr G F Young, who once lived at the abbey, the boundaries of these landmarks were in existence 'until about 1934 when the property was acquired by the late Mr Herbert Carter of Holbeach'. He also states that at that time there was also a stone tablet built into the west wall bearing the letters 'I.L.F. 1607'. These stood for John and Frances Lockton, who built the house in 1607. There was also a stone figure of a knight in armour set into the east wall of the house. Young records that the original well of the abbey, seventy feet deep, and 'magnificently lined with large dressed stone blocks', supplied the house with water.

The Great Retting Pits were for the retting and processing of flax which was grown on land belonging to the abbey. These pits would be about four feet deep and full of water. The flax was harvested, tied into sheaves which were packed into the retting pits, then submerged and held down with stones to prevent them floating. They were left there for seven - fourteen days during which time fermentation took place, releasing the fibres. The fibres were then dried in the fields and later spun into linen.

The layout of the house can be imagined from the will of William

Lockton.

'William Lockton of Swineshead Abbey, esq. 2nd Oct 1657.

I give to Ann my wife in lieu of her Dowry the Rooms I now live in commonly called Swineshead Abbey; that is all the Rooms in the Dairy Court that my son John lived in, with the Chamber over the old Kitchen, the Dairy House and Rooms over it, part of the Cellar House from the Entry unto the North End of the Half Cellar, so much of the Stable that my son John had; also the ground and pastures, the Garden, the ground called the Crow Park, both the Deer Parks, the Pasture called Eastlings and pasture called Pinchbeck, and after her death to my daughter by her, Elizabeth and her heirs. To my daughter Rose the Farm and House late in the tenure of Francis Harris Widow, now let to Joseph Harris and in tenure of John Maultby, so long as she remain unmarried. If she marry with the consent of my supervisor Basil Beridge then to her heirs, but if she marry without his consent, then the above land and House to go to my son John and his heirs. I give her also the Bakehouse for a Kitchen and the Lime House for a Dairy. To my son John the Manor of Swineshead bought of Sir John Woldenholme, as largely as the Knight sold it to me, and to my son's heirs; also the other Rooms in the Abbey; and after his death to his son John and his heirs. Wife and daughter Rose executrixes. Supervisors my friend Basil Beridge, Rector of Algarkirk, my cousin Thomas Pinchbeck of Boston and my Cousin William Balderston a seal ring each value 40s inscribed 'Fides in eternum.'

Witnesses, Basil Beridge, Alice Ebbeston, and Robert Harrison.

Proved PCC 8 Feb 1657/8 by the executrixes.'

William Lockton was buried at Swineshead on the 6th of October.

William's daughter Rose married Thomas Dickenson at Swineshead church on October 7th 1658, just a year after her father's death. It would be interesting to know if she married with or without the permission of Basil Berridge.

(William was one of the signatories to orders made during the visitation of the plague in 1636. See appendix).

On William's death the abbey estate passed to his eldest surviving son, John. John married Frances Humphreys at Pinchbeck on 6th November 1649, and they had three sons; Thomas born 1652 who predeceased his father, William baptised December 1654 and who died a fortnight later, and John also baptised in 1654. There were three daughters Audrey, Mary and Elizabeth.

On John's death, his son John (bapt 1654) inherited the estate. This John also married a Frances — circa 1670. She may have been his half-cousin Frances Lockton, born 1654, the daughter of John Lockton of Drayton Hall.

John and Frances had three sons, John, Robert, and Ferdinand.

Their father died in 1680, whilst his children were still young. His will dated 7th January 1679/80, after the usual preliminaries reads as follows:

> It: I give to my beloved wife Frances Lockton in lieu of her dowry the priviledge of the foreyard and the use of the well in it and the swineyard with the house in it and the dairy court, the dairy in it, and the lowe room next unto it with the chambers over it and the kitchen chamber with the chambers over it, and all those grounds the garden where the ewe tree stands and the orchards where the -?- pear tree stands and the use of the Brew House all which sd premises are situate and lie in Swineshead aforesd during a whole year after my decease and after I give all the romes and grounds unto my sonne John Lockton and his heirs of his body lawfully and for want of any heirs then to my sons Robert and to his heirs and for want to same of to Ferdinand and his heirs.
>
> It: I give to Frances Lockton my wife all those pastures called Eastings containing by estimation 20 acres lying in Swineshead afsd to be sold by her as soon as maybe, for and towards the payment of Mr Goodhands mortgages.
>
> It: I give to my son Robert Lockton those grounds that is

to say the pasture called Conihills and the pastures called Pincbecke, pastures called Crow Pasture, the Little Boare Park, all lying in Swineshead aforesd and to heirs of his bodie and then to son Ferdinand and the heirs of his body.

It: I give to my son Ferdinand the Great Deer Park, Fould Green with the rigge with them all lying in Swineshead and his heirs and for want of same then to my son Robert and his heirs.

Item: I give to my son John my manor belonging to Swineshead Abbey with all other my lands and tenements not given before and to his heirs.

It: I give to John Orme my little horse called Barlly [Barley] and my silver rapier.

Rest of goods and chattels to Frances my wife, my sole executrix.'

So the manor of Swineshead Abbey passed to young John Lockton, then aged about ten years, in July 1680. The date of John's birth or baptism is not known, but the baptismal dates of his younger brothers Robert 1672, and Ferdinand 1674, suggest that he was born about 1670. Frances, their mother was still living, and probably because her eldest son was still a minor she was appointed sole executor.

John only survived his father by sixteen weeks, when his brother Robert may have succeeded. Robert would only have been eight years old. There is no trace of marriage or issue and Robert may also have died young. The third son, Ferdinand died at the age of twenty-two, presumably unmarried, as their is no record of marriage or issue. At this point, 1697, the male Lockton line in Swineshead appears to have died out, as neither uncles nor cousins were living. (See the Locktons genealogical chart in the appendix).

This assumption is given credence, not only by the recorded family tree, but by the fact that (according to Marrat writing in 1813) the estate ended up in Chancery, from whence it was purchased, at some unstated future date.

The Ross Mss record that the Abbey farm was the seat of John

Cotton esq in 1733.

According to the same Mss, the estate was purchased, in 1733, by John Asgill, a Member of Parliament, jointly with Sir Cleve More. Several litigations followed, involving Dame Osbaston and Sophia More, relict of Sir Joseph Edmonds More, which suggests that the ownership was still being contested.

In May 1739 a survey was taken of the Abbey Farm which gave the acreage as 125 acres 2 roods 31 perches. Holt Hill Farm containing 52 acres 1 rood 25 perches was also part of the estate. Names of the fields and other areas surveyed were 'Dove Coat Close, Yards, and Abbey Walk, Coney Hills, Pare Tree Piece, Little Dear Park, Great Dear Park, Little Three Acres, Little Acre, Low Five Acres, Eastings, Woodheads, Hartley Green, Lath Close, Beacon Close, Butcher's Close, Lord's Orchard, Nutt Tree Piece, Mear Close, Abbey Lane, Abbey Drove.'

In 1737 Samuel Reynardson was the tenant, and he appears to have been in possession in 1777, before the property passed to Jacob Reynardson, who was probably his son. According to the Honourable John Byng, fifth Viscount Torrington, on his tour through England in 1791, an 'old fat farmer' then lived at the abbey. John Byng doesn't give the name of the farmer, but he may have been Jacob Reynardson, who did not die until 1806.

The farmer showed the Viscount where he thought the old priory had stood. He took him into the garden and pointed out the stump of a famous yew tree that marked the place where the sea once reached, the trunk of which tree had been sold to a miller for £20, for a mill post. He also showed him a stone figure of a knight in armour fixed on the outside of the house wall. Apparently as a boy the farmer used to shoot at it with a pistol, and caused damaged to the nose of the figure. The farmer said that he intended to repair it one day, but he clearly did not as the damaged nose remains. He further stated that when he had once buried some cattle that had died of 'distemper', he must have accidentally dug in the old burial ground of the monks, as he dug up some human skeletons.

According to Marrat, the abbey was purchased, circa 1813, by J

G Calthrop Esq of Gosberton. The Calthrop family lived there for some years. In 1825 during the construction of a well in the grounds of the abbey, the skeleton of a man measuring six feet four inches in height was unearthed.

In 1846 Herbert Ingram, the founder of *The Illustrated London News*, purchased the Abbey from the Calthrop family. Mr Ingram spent a considerable amount of money improving the property, erecting splendid new iron gates at the southern entrance, and some fine wooden ones at the western gateway. He also planted many new trees, including three Austrian oaks.

A farmer called Frederick Curtois and his family were the occupiers of the abbey in 1876, presumably renting it from the Ingram family. The Curtois family later moved to Brothertoft Hall.

In 1860 Herbert Ingram died and the Abbey passed into the ownership of his son, Sir William James Ingram, who lived in Westgate-on-Sea. In 1882 Sir William employed George Frederick Young as the resident agent of his Lincolnshire estates, and the Young family moved into the Abbey farmhouse. The Youngs lived at the Abbey from 1882 to 1922. According to George Young junior, in a letter to the Boston Standard in 1971, the abbey was of considerable size in 1922, having seven large double bedrooms on the first floor, three large bedrooms on the second floor and two bathrooms.

Realising his childhood ambition, George Frederick Young, junior, bought the Abbey from Sir William Ingram in 1920. He later sold it to Mr William Gilding of Swineshead on condition that he could buy it back, should Mr Gilding ever wish to sell it. However Mr Gilding died suddenly, and unknown to Mr Young it came on to the market, subsequently being purchased by Mr H P Carter of Holbeach.

Mr Young tried to buy the abbey farmhouse from Mr Carter but was unsuccessful. It remained in the possession of the Carter family for some years, during which time the old house was turned into three or four farm workers dwellings. It was used as such for a while, but was afterwards left empty and allowed to fall into decay.

8. Abbey Road looking towards the church, early this century.

In 1971 the Carters applied for permission to demolish the old abbey farmhouse built by Sir John Lockton, as it was in such a bad state of repair. Local people however were most distressed at the idea. Mrs Winifred Crunkhorn wrote to the Daily Mail newspaper explaining the dilemma, outlining the history of the abbey, and appealing for some help to prevent what she considered would be a disaster. As a result there appeared in The Daily Mail, on Friday 28th May 1971, an article about the abbey on the lines of 'time is running out' saying how scandalous it would be to demolish something with as much history as Swineshead Abbey.

An officer from RAF Leconfield, near Beverley in Yorkshire, read the article in the newspaper and offered to buy the abbey farmhouse. On finding out just what it would cost to renovate the property, he decided against the purchase, but by then the demolition order had already been cancelled, and the abbey was saved.

The Abbey Farm Estate was eventually sold in 1972. The estate then included the farm manager's house; Sykemouth farmhouse; Creasey Plot farmhouse; a pair of modern bungalows at Swineshead North End; the Abbey Farm bungalow; Thorpe's Cottage; and 890 acres of farmland. There were also three sets of farm buildings. The house and parkland were sold separately some years later.

After having changed hands twice more, the old house has now been restored by the present owner, and it is once more a family home.

Note: The Cistercian abbey was totally destroyed in 1536. The stones were then used by Sir John Lockton to build himself a house on the site in 1607. This house, once derelict but now restored as a family home, is still referred to as 'The Abbey' or 'Swineshead Abbey'. Any references in this text to 'the Abbey' after 1607 relate to the house.

NEITHER THE HOUSE NOR THE GROUNDS ARE OPEN TO THE PUBLIC.

Chapter Three

Churches and Chapels

Eʀʟʏ Cʜʀɪsᴛɪᴀɴ sᴇʀᴠɪᴄᴇs ɪɴ Eɴɢʟᴀɴᴅ were commonly held in the open air at sites usually marked by a stone cross. Some early crosses were erected as boundary markers or at cross roads, but others marked the place where missionaries would preach. A market, or butter cross, usually served a different purpose being in the centre of a village, usually the market place, when its purpose was to put the village and its commerce under the protection of Christ. In many instances the one cross served both purposes.

9. Stump Cross.
(What appears to be the
base is modern, not original)

Swineshead has Stump Cross, which now stands in South Street at the junction with Stump Cross Lane; and the Market Cross, the remains of which still stand in the Market Place. Stump Cross is a shaft without a base, and the market cross is a base without a shaft.

The Stump Cross measures thirteen inches square across the lower part of its shaft (square in section and not tapering) and the Market Cross measures fourteen and a half inches across the square socket where its shaft once fitted. As the stone of both these monuments is most uneven, these measurements are not precise. Even so it would seem likely that the one could fit into the other, and an earlier writer (Green) also pointed out that the shaft of the Stump Cross and the base of the Market

41.

Cross are of the same type of stone.

In 1565 during the Reformation, a Colonel Hollingworth was sent to Swineshead with his men to 'destroy all superstitious articles'. He took down two old altars in the church, one of which was broken in the act. In view of the instructions given to Colonel Hollingworth it is quite conceivable that the market cross was pulled down at the same time. It would only need two or three men on horseback with ropes tied around the cross to pull the shaft from the base and possibly drag it along the road before abandoning it.

Stump Cross is not on its original site, and it is claimed that it has been moved from earlier locations twice. Marrat writing in 1813 says that it 'stands in the road leading to Bicker a little way from the church'. On the 1904 OS map it is shown as standing in a field by Packhorse Lane. According to Green, in his village

10. The stocks and the base of the old butter cross in the Market Place. This early photograph shows the lower part of the broken shaft still in place at that time.

42.

history of 1913, the shaft of the cross standing beside the Packhorse Road was 'simply planted directly in the earth' and had no base.

The foregoing facts do seem to point to Stump Cross and the Market Cross being parts of an original whole.

Some years ago when the old Market Cross or Butter Cross was being restored by C A Woods of Spilsby, an even older base of the cross was discovered. After examination it was claimed that this possible original base was about 1000 years old. This pre-dates both the abbey and the church, and this monument may have been the base of an early preaching cross. (An old village well with part of its pump was uncovered nearby at the same time, but this was only about one hundred years old).

It eventually became the custom to build a church somewhere near the preaching cross to enable services to be held in comfort during bad weather. (This is another reason to suppose that the cross in the market place was also the preaching cross). Early churches built before 1066 had only a nave and chancel. Originally the congregation in the church would remain standing, but towards the later Middle Ages seating was introduced. Churches began to be more elaborate, and during the medieval period narrow aisles were built either side of the nave.

In the eleventh century parish churches were being founded by wealthy landowners who paid for the building of the church and endowed it with land (glebeland), and a house for the priest. The landowner then had the advowson of the church, i.e. he had the right to appoint a priest of his choice.

These early churches were often built of wood and needed constant maintenance. Whilst the priest had the income from the glebeland it was also necessary to levy 'tithes' for the upkeep of the church.

Tithes were introduced by the Anglo Saxons. Every man in the village was expected to pay a tenth of all his produce/income to support the church. Tithe barns were erected to hold the corn and other such produce collected.

It is believed that Swineshead church was first dedicated in

1219, although a church probably existed before then, as there is a record of Alan de Croun making a donation in the early twelfth century to 'the church of Saints Salvador and Mary and the market there'. The donation consisted of one oxgang and a half of land at Burton Pedwardine. [Alan de Croun held the manor of Freiston, and founded a priory there for Benedictine monks.]

Another early mention of the church occurs when the abbot of Swineshead procured the King's licence to hold a fair at the Chapel of St Saviour in Swineshead 'in the 20th year of Edward' (1292).

In October of 1919, on the first Sunday in the month, the 700th anniversary of the dedication of Swineshead church was celebrated. This would not have been the present church, as it wasn't built until the fourteenth century.

In the early 13th century chapels of ease or parochial chapels were established in outlying areas of parishes. The patron of the parish church was entitled to restrict the services that were allowed at these chapels and claim a right to the tithes. If he neglected to do so, then such a chapel could claim to be a 'free chapel'. This is probably what happened at St Adrian's Chapel at Barthorpe in Swineshead.

The earliest mention of the Chapel of St Adrian is by Bishop Grossteste when, in 1239-40, Adam de Aston, the chaplain, resigned to become Rector of the church of Swineshead, and was replaced by one Roger − −.

The next chaplain was William de Gimes who died circa 1286. He was followed by Richard de Stamford, who was appointed by Lady Hawisa de Grelle, who was the patron of the chapel at that time.

The revenues of this chapel then consisted of 'the receipt of two parts of the tithe of sheaves and hay issuing from the demesne lands belonging to the said Manor of Swynesheued,' and also 'two parts of the tithe of wool and lambs issuing from the same Manor.' Revenues also consisted of the oblations made in the chapel and income from eight acres of land, valued at 13s per annum.

In his register, dated July 1293, Bishop Oliver Sutton records a 'Mandate to the sequestrator in the deanery of Holland to deliver to

Master Reginald of Wakerley, rector of the Chapel of Swineshead, certain books which Richard the last rector had given to the said chapel, and which, since he died intestate, had been sequestrated along with his other goods.' The books were returned and the gift confirmed 'before witnesses' on July 16th 1293.

Reginald of Wakerley had been instated on 29th June of that year. He was not chaplain for very long, as another entry in Bishop Sutton's register records on the 9th November 1293 that John de Southover was instated at the death of Reginald of Wakerley. Five years later, in 1298, Bishop Sutton records a mandate to suspend the sentence of excommunication of the servants of Sir William of Swineshead, chaplain.

The last known chaplain of St Adrians was Robert Smyth in 1535. In 1552 the Abbey site was granted to Admiral Lord Clinton, and this possibly included the chapel. According to Rev Cragg, this chapel fell into decay but was still standing in 1684.

The exact location of St Adrian's Chapel is not known. Rev Cragg says 'No doubt it stood on the site now known as Chapel Field.' This may be so, but there seems to be no proof of this. 'Chapel Ground' is identified on the 1904 O.S. map as a field lying a few hundred yards north east of the junction of Blackjack Road and the A52. In fairly recent times human bones were unearthed there when the field was being cultivated. This is an indication that a burial ground existed there, and possibly a chapel.

The first mention of a priest at the parish church of Sts Saviour and Mary is in 1290, when Bishop Sutton notes in his register that the order to sequestrate the property of the church in Swineshead was to be relaxed. This order had been made because of the 'non-residence of Master John the rector'. Master John was fined one mark instead. This incident happened before the present church was built.

Some time during the fourteenth century, a stone church was built by the side of the Swin to replace the original one, which would have been made of wood. The stone to build the church probably came from Barnack in Northamptonshire and would have been brought by boat up the Swin and unloaded at the spot where

45.

the church was to be built.

This must have been a very fine church for its time. A large church pre-supposes a large congregation and suggests wealthy patrons. The Grelley and de la Warre families were the early patrons and the church once contained some stained glass windows with the arms of these families, but unfortunately these no longer exist.

In 1833 Lord Monson, when travelling around Lincolnshire, described Swineshead church as being 'very handsome'. He described the nave and aisles as being decorated on each side by six pointed arches, the westernmost arch of the south aisle being blocked up, as it was at this time being used as a school. A school was still being held in the church in 1848 according to the Rev Holmes. The comments of Lord Monson and Rev Holmes indicate that a school or class was held in the church long after two classrooms had been built on land purchased by the trustees of Cowley's Charity in February 1825.

Monson went on to say that the benching in the church was ancient, although some of it was still good, but the pulpit was painted 'a flaming brick colour'. The small chapel was blocked up and in use as a lumber room, and the floor of the nave was covered in boarding which hid the stones beneath. Some of the windows were unglazed and falling in, and the church generally seemed to have been in a poor condition at this time.

In 1847 the chancel of the church was rebuilt under the direction of Mr Stephen Lewin, an architect from Boston. It was similar in style to the original one, which was 15th century. This restoration was funded by Trinity College, Cambridge, which had the advowson at this time. The church had been neglected for some time and was said to be in a deplorable state, the roof being open to the weather and allowing access to birds. The cost of this work was £2000.

On Jan 6th 1848 a service was held by the vicar, Rev H L Guilleband, to mark the opening of the new chancel, and a sermon was preached by Rev J H Oldrid of Boston. Some 200 Sunday School children attended the service and afterwards walked in procession to the schoolroom where they were given a meal of roast beef and plum pudding, by courtesy of Trinity College.

In 1865, the Stamford Mercury reported that during that year's severe winter Swineshead church had been without heating. Recent fundraising had been regrettably inadequate and since the last organist had left the parish the organ had been locked up as 'there are no funds to raise the wind'. The article went on to say that the sexton, a man of over 80, had had his salary reduced by £1 'after years of looking after both the living and the dead'.

The church was again in need of some attention and on May 5th 1868, some further restoration began. The nave was lowered by fourteen inches to its original level, and three blocks of new seating of carved English oak were fitted. These were carved in keeping with the remaining original block of old seating, which had been carefully repaired. The floor was relaid in Ancaster stone and plaster and paint was removed from the walls. Most of the windows were reglazed. The architect for this project was Mr Kirk of Sleaford.

To pay for this renovation of 1868, listed subscribers had paid a total of £1287.4.5d, which was spent as follows:

PAYMENTS

	£.	s.	d.
Franks, stonemason	516	6	7
Pattinson, seating	444	17	0
Payne, plumber and glazier	65	7	10
Tuxfordd, ditto	28	10	6
Morriss, carpenter	38	3	11
Woods, blacksmith	18	14	8
Walker, ditto	17	4	6
Mason, ditto	2	13	0
Osgarby, ditto	3	2	4
Morton, printer	6	11	10
Bagg, hire of carts and horses	1	13	6
S Dawson, work at church	1	12	0
Brindley, moving old organ	8	0	0

Wright, ironmonger	0	5	3
Byron, nails, brushes, &c.	1	1	8
Jones and Willis, curtains for doors	20	3	9
Ditto, matting for floor	8	18	4
Jackson, hire of omnibus, Oct 14th	3	0	0
Advertisements in newspapers	5	17	8
Labourers, lowering floor of Church, &c	15	8	9
Expenses of choir from Spalding	12	1	0
Eight Ringers	2	0	0
Pattinson's men	1	0	0
Stephenson, cart hire	0	10	6
Carriage of parcels	1	2	10
Expenses at sale of old materials	0	12	0
Man distributing bills	0	3	9
Moss, License to hold service in School	2	2	0
Swan, Faculty to restore Church	6	0	0
Kirk, architect	49	11	8
Postage, stationery, &c	4	7	7
	£1287	4	5
Received	£1292	1	9
Paid	£1287	4	5
	£4	17	4

(The above account was taken from a pamphlet - *Restoration of St Mary's Church, Swineshead, Lincolnshire 1868-1869'*)

Despite all this building work, completed in October, the roof still needed repairing and the porch was in a dilapidated state.

As part of the 1868 restoration Mr William Dolby Reddish, one of the churchwardens, donated a new organ, built by Brindley of Sheffield. He also gave gas fittings and two new stoves, a pulpit and prayer desk and a hundred chairs, and cushions and hassocks for all the seating, and money to repair the bells. The vicar, Canon Joseph Holmes, was responsible for restoring the font and gave a new altar, a stone credence table and an alms box. He also provided for the pavement tiles in the baptistry.

The ladies of the parish presented a new altar cloth and a dossel hanging, kneeling mats for the altar and font, an embroidered velvet frontal for the pulpit and some book markers embroidered in gold. Colonel Moore, of Frampton Hall, donated an oak lectern, Mr Jessop of Nottingham, presented a white linen cover for the altar, and Mr Kirk gave the carved work on the chancel screen.

An ancient altar slab found in the floor of the nave, was moved to a new place on the floor in front of the altar. Canon Holmes, the vicar, had read about this old altar in an account of the despoiling of Swineshead church during the Reformation, and had determined to find it if he could. This altar slab was one of two original altars which were taken down in 1565, by Colonel Martin Hollingworth. The preserved slab was laid in the floor of the nave to form part of the paving, the other one was unfortunately broken. The existing altar stone has been estimated to be at least 1,000 years old. (Some years later it was moved again, this time being leant against the wall under the east window of the south aisle. Today it forms the altar table there).

Services were held on Thursday 14th October 1869 to dedicate the new work. The morning sermon was preached by the Right Reverend Dr Christopher Wordsworth, Lord Bishop of Lincoln, and the evening service was conducted by Reverend Francis Charles Massingberd MA, Chancellor. The Archdeacon of Stow and forty-five other clergy were present along with a large congregation.

Fifteen years later, in 1884, the spire was struck by lightning, but there does not appear to have been any substantial damage.

Before 1794 the church had only four bells, two of which may have been cast before the middle of the sixteenth century. These two bore latin inscriptions, one of which translated as: 'May the bell of John sound for many years', and the other: 'Hail Mary, full of grace, the Lord is with thee, blessed art thou among women and blessed is thy offspring'.

In 1794 a peal of eight new bells was cast by Thomas Osborn of Downham Market, Norfolk. On the treble or first bell is inscribed 'Percute duce cano. Wm. Ellis subscriber'. On the second and fourth bells the inscription is 'T. Osborn fecit', whilst the seventh bell has a similar 'Thos. Osborn fecit Downham, 1794'. The third bell carries the words 'Cum voco venite'; the fifth bell, 'In wedlock's bands all ye who join/ With hands your hearts unite/ So shall our tuneful tongues combine/ To laud the nuptial rite'; the sixth bell, 'Our voices shall in concert ring/ In honour both to God and King';

and the eighth or tenor bell, 'Robert Uvedale, D.D., Vicar. Joseph Mason, Wm. Brewster, Ch. Wardens'. A dedication service was held on June 10th 1794 (Whit Tuesday) when the bells were rung by a renowned team of bellringers from Norwich.

In 1883 four of these bells were recast by Taylor's of Loughborough, and in 1922 the tenor bell was recast by Meeres and Stainbanks of London.

In 1926-37 further restoration work took place, when the bells were rehung and the nave roof was repaired. A heating system was installed at the same time.

In 1948 a local newspaper reported that 'cracks in the spire of Swineshead Parish Church have been caused by the corrosion of the iron rod (dowelled into the masonry) which supports the weather vane. For its repair the masonry will have to be cut away and a non-ferrous rod fixed.' The

11. *Mr Thomas Hinkins, sexton, sitting on one of the church bells at the time of their restoration during the 1920s and 1930s.*

spire was eventually repaired in 1951, costing £1000. The chantry chapel, along with the south aisle, was restored in 1952.

In 1988 an appeal was launched to restore the church yet again. Today English Heritage and The Historic Churches Preservation Trust are both helping towards this end.

Today, visitors entering the church by the west door will notice above the door a stained glass window showing the Infant Saviour being worshipped by the magi. This window is dedicated to William Dolby Reddish.

On the west wall, near the door, is a large board headed BENEFACTIONS which lists people who have left land and/or property for various good causes. John Dickenson left eight acres of pasture land, the rent of which was to be distributed among the poor. Thomas Dickenson left a cottage, a yard and half an acre of pasture; Henry Pridgeon left twenty acres of pasture land; and William Hart in 1699 gave to the poor of Swineshead a windmill, two cottages, some land near Tarry Hill and also some land in the Town Field. Robert Woolmer gave two acres of pasture land in Bicker, the money from which was to be for the preaching of four sermons a year; and John Butler left 'one Messuage, Barn, Stable, Out Houses, Garden, Yard, and Five Acres of Arable Land .... in Swineshead' and one and a half acres of pasture in Wigtoft in trust for the repairs to the 'Causeways belonging to the said Parish of Swineshead.' More details of these will be given in a later chapter dealing with Swineshead Charities.

Near the door in the wall of the north aisle the visitor will see an ancient stone coffin of unknown age. Past this original door, which dates from the fifteenth century, on the north wall of the aisle can be seen tablets of white marble on a black base. These are memorials to Margaret Bellairs, who died in 1839, and to James Bellairs, her husband, formerly of London, who died in Rippingale in 1849; William Barnes, who died in 1846; and Mary his widow, who died in 1860. Also on the north wall is a tablet to James Jessop, who died in 1840 aged 35, 'suddenly and awfully deprived of life by the accidental discharge of a gun'.

The organ, which was originally built by Brindley of Sheffield,

*12. St. Mary's Church around one hundred years ago.
— a view about the turn of the century.*

13. St Mary's Parish Church as it is today— 1996.

was rebuilt in 1961 by Messrs T L Jubb & Son of Gainsborough. Near the organ is a tablet on the east wall of the north aisle, commemorating John Willerton of Swineshead who died in 1841. Nearby in the floor is a memorial to Richard Benet and his wife, dated 1520. This stone has some small holes cut into its surface. It has been suggested that this may have been done by the children for use in a game. At one time the village school was held in the nave and the children would play in the graveyard, or in the church if it was raining.

The pulpit, no longer flame red as in Monson's time, is on the left of the chancel. On the right is a fine lectern in the shape of an eagle. On the wall behind the lectern there is a white marble plaque dedicated to Canon Joseph Holmes MA, who died on November 8th 1911. He was the longest serving vicar of Swineshead, being the incumbent there for 63 years.

The rood screen dates from the fifteenth century. Beyond it in the chancel, on the right of the vestry door, can be seen the memorial to Sir John Lockton which reads:

NERE THIS PLACE DOTH LYE THE BODDY OF Sr IOHN LOCKTON KNIGHT WHOE DEPARTED THIS LIFE IN THE 56th YEARE OF HIS AGE UPON THE 9th DAY OF IANUARY IN THE YEARE OF OUR REDEMTION 1610 WHOE HAD BY DAME FRANCIS HIS WIFE A 11 CHILDREN THREE ONLY LIVING, WILLIAM, IOHN AND FRANCIS WHICH DAME FRANCIS YET SURVIVING AT HER ONNE COST AND CHARGES IN TOKEN OF HER LOVE AND TO THE LIVING MEMORY OF HER DECEASED HUSBAND HATH ERECTED THIS MONUMENT
ANNO DOMINI
1628

Underneath this plaque is a row of carved figures of the eleven children. Those who died in infancy are depicted as babes in the cradle. The older children who had died before 1628 are depicted each holding a skull.

In 1843 there was a further inscription below this which is no longer there. It read:

'What epitaph shall we afford this shrine?
Words cannot grace this monument of thine:
His sweet perfections summed up were such
As Heaven, I think, for earth did think too much.
Honest, religious, wise; so good a liver.
He lived to die, and died to live forever.
Then let each Christian's heart join with my pen
To embalm his virtues in the minds of men.'

Behind the choir stalls there is a hidden entrance to a crypt possibly the one belonging to the Lockton family. It contains five coffins.

Behind the altar is a large stained glass window with the inscription 'In memory of Joseph Mason Tenant of Leeds he died April 1872 Aged 74 years and rests in peace in the graveyard here.'

On the east wall of the south aisle is a memorial tablet to Rev William Bolland MA, Vicar of Swineshead for 29 years, who died in 1840. On the east wall of the aisle is a memorial tablet to Elizabeth, his first wife, where the vicar is described as being the vicar of both Swineshead and Frampton. It reads:

```
Sacred
to the memory of
Elizabeth
wife of the Revd. Wm Bolland M.A.
Vicar of Swineshead and Frampton
and late fellow of Trinity College Cambridge
who departed this life on the 21 day of March 1817
in the 26 year of her age
with a well grounded hope of a glorious immortality.
```

Nearby is another to Sarah his second wife as follows:

In memory of
Sarah second wife of the
Revd Will Bolland M.A. Vicar of this parish
who entered upon her eternal rest
March 1827 in the 42 year of her age.
Her only hope was the finished work of
our Lord Jesus Christ which supported her
protracted bodily afflictions
Gave her the Victory over her last enemy
and at length brought her to the full
'fruition of the glorious Godhead'
Three of her children who died in their
infancy are also interred with her
in a vault near
this place.

Between these tablets is a memorial window 'To the Glory of God and in memory of relatives laid to rest in the churchyard by Charles Arthur Tennant 1892'. Along the east wall under this window is the ancient altar slab forming the top of the small altar there.

A window on the south wall of the aisle has an inscription 'In loving memory of Jonathan Garlick, who is buried at Algarkirk, and Elizabeth Charlotte, his wife, who is buried in Johannesburg, South Africa; and also of Richard Hides and Mary Caswell his wife, buried in Swineshead. These are the parents and grandparents of John Garlick, who dedicated the window to them and many other members of the Garlick family recorded in the parish registers from 1653-1901.' Near this window is a tablet to the memory of William Bolland, Vicar of this Parish.

Another window on the south wall of the nave is dedicated to Canon Holmes and his wife. The inscription reads 'In beloved memory of Joseph Holmes Canon of Lincoln Cathedral and Vicar of this Parish from 1848 to 1911, died November 8th 1911 in his

91st year and of Frances Caroline his wife, died August 31st 1907 in her 75th year.'

The wooden flooring on this side of the church is suffering badly from the woodworm and part of it is fenced off with a notice warning the public of the danger.

Near the fourteenth century south door is a wooden board with the names of local men lost in the Great War. Beneath it is a smaller one to those who died in the Second World War.

In the south west corner of the church is the baptistry where the plain octagonal font stands on a tiled floor. This floor was laid during the restoration of 1868, when Canon Holmes was responsible for both the laying of these tiles and the restoration of the font.

The nave dates from the fourteenth century, although some of the roof timbers date from the sixteenth century, and it has six north and south arcades. At the top of the pillars can be seen numerous small head carvings. On the floor of the nave can be seen slabs to the memory of past vicars of Swineshead. One reads: Here lyeth the/ bodie of/ Iohn Iennings/ late vicar/ of Swineshead/ who departed/ this life/ June ye 4th 1715. Another is to Thomas Maddocks, also a vicar of Swineshead, who died on the 18th March 1728. His wife Mary who died on 31st July 1726, is also buried nearby.

High up on the east wall of the nave, above the rood screen are two small stained glass windows. There are seven stained glass windows in the church, all the rest being of clear glass.

Outside the church can be seen many more carved heads. Of particular interest are the ones along the outer walls of the chancel. On the north wall of the chancel are the heads of a knight and his lady, and high above these are a flying cow and a boar's head. Either side of the stained glass window on the east wall of the chancel, are the heads of a king and a bishop, and above these a flying lion. Round the corner along the south wall of the chancel are various clearly defined heads including another king, and a soldier.

On the tower, is a clock bearing the date 1767, the mechanism for which was rebushed in 1952. The tower, which dates from the fifteenth century and is 160 feet high, contains eight bells. These bells were cast in 1794, but before this there were four only, two of them being cast before the Reformation. The curfew was tolled from October to March at 8 o'clock every evening for five minutes, followed by a short interval when another bell was rung to indicate the date of the month. This was still happening in 1898 and possibly until more recent times. (The curfew was a regulation in medieval times whereby 'at a fixed hour in the evening, indicated by the ringing of a bell, fires were to be covered over and extinguished'. It has nothing to do with the Danes, as local legend suggests). The spire was added to the tower some time in the sixteenth century.

A bench seat by the south door is dedicated to Dorothy Ellen Oliver who died on February 1st 1972 aged 74.

In the aisle there is a board containing a list of the past vicars of Swineshead. (See appendix).

The longest serving vicar of Swineshead was Canon Joseph Holmes who was vicar there for nearly 64 years. He was aged 90 when he died, and was buried in Swineshead churchyard on November 11th 1911. He was responsible for the building of the old Swineshead vicarage. The Canon had a large family of daughters, Caroline, Isabel, Alice, Katharine, Cecilia and Charlotte, who were all still living at home unmarried in 1881, despite all being over the age of 18. As well as this large family, there was also Canon Holmes' sister Juliana and three live-in servants. It was not surprising that he felt the need to build himself a large vicarage. A new vicarage was built in 1981.

Another recent vicar of note is Rev J G H Cragg whose induction took place in 1938, The Lincolnshire Standard reported that Rev Cragg was presented with a clock by Mr Scott of Sleaford on behalf of the choir boys of St Denys Church, Sleaford, where he had been curate. Rev Cragg was vicar of Swineshead for 38 years, and was a local amateur historian, being responsible for a booklet on the history of Swineshead.

Other long serving vicars were Francis Gough who served for 45 years between 1715 and 1760; Robert Uvedale, who followed him in 1760 and stayed until 1800; William Bolland, 1811 to 1840;

and Thomas Garten who was priest in Swineshead in 1508/9 for 28 years.

Swineshead parish records date back to 1561. The following are the first few entries in the registers.

PARISH REGISTERS

Swynhead
A register taken of all the
chrytenings maryages and Buryalls
from the first of Sainte Mychaell
th arckangell in the yere of o'r lord
god 1561 by the churche wardens Thome
hall & Thomas Yorke.

Xpistsyngs

Octobiat	Sarah Wytham	6 daye
	rose Operwax	6 daye
	Thome Simson	12 daye
	Thomas Gawdale	12 daye
	Jane Gawdale	26 daye
Novbs	Danyell Gaule	8 daye
	rychard Laker	8 daye
	Ales massengbery	20 daye
	Ales rolate	20 daye
Decc	Matthew Sanderson	16 daye
	Annes Sallomon	16 daye

Buryalls

October	Annye farme	— daye
Novb	Wyllm browne	28 daye
Decb	maude browne	5 daye
	Jane browne	5 daye
	Wyllyam meloc	20 daye
March	Thomas —	4 daye
	Andrew rychardson	6 daye
	Daniell woolmer	20 daye
	George ryecrofte	28 daye

| | Annye Sallomon | 30 daye |
| | Ales massengberye | 30 daye |

Maryages

October	robarte browne & margy clarke	20 daye
Janyary	Wm hansop & margy wytlam	21 daye
	Edward lockett & Elizabeth poole	24 daye
Apryll	Wm taylor & Elizabeth pawllin	20 daye
Maye	Matthew browne & an blesbery	4 daye
Augt	Roger Booteyer & Jane rycrofte	12 daye

per me Johne bollingsleye curate de Swinshed.

Among more recent entries, and indicative of views at that time, is the tragic one entered by Canon Holmes.

| 1865 Dec 8th | Charles Herd (felo de se) buried between 9 and 12 o'clock at night, without Christian Rites. J H. (Felo de se = committed suicide). |

Other similar entries made by Canon Holmes include:

| 1874 Feb 4th | Sarah Ann Wanty. Swineshead. 28 years. sibi necem conscierit. J H. (committed suicide). |

| 1879 Apr 29th | Charles Porter, Gibbet Hills near Swineshead. 54 years. sibi ipse necem in fluvio conscivit. J H> (killed himself in the river). |

| 1881 Feb 17th | William Redman. Swineshead. 65 years. Mann sua periit. J H. (drowned by his own hand). |

| 1886 Aug 17th | William Walton (Hofflete) Swineshead. 72 years. necem sibi ipse consivit. |

| 1891 Mar 5th | Joseph Love Swineshead. 40 years. mortem sibi ipse conscivit. J H. |

It is not stated whether or not these last five people were buried at night.

60.

There were other places of worship in the village besides St Mary's. In the nineteenth century Swineshead also had three chapels. In 1896, according to White's Directory, there were the Baptist, the Wesleyan, and the Free Methodist chapels, and in the previous year a Mission Room had been built at North End.

The Methodist Chapel, which stood in High Street, dated from 1845, but was replaced in 1908 by another building which stood next door to the old one. This new chapel cost £1,650 to build. The opening ceremony took place on 12th March 1908, and Mrs T J Rayson of Nottingham and Mrs J W Skinner of Boston officiated. In 1920 a piped organ was installed and dedicated to the memory of those who died in the first World War. In 1950 this organ was rebuilt and the dedication ceremony was attended by Sandy Macpherson of the BBC, who was a famous organist of the time.

In 1986 the old Methodist Chapel (dated 1845) was demolished brick by brick by Tony Johnson, a local business man, and the materials were used by him in the building of his bungalow, Norton Lodge, on the opposite side of the road.

The Wesleyan Chapel was in South Street where the fish and chip shop now stands and was demolished earlier this century.

The Baptist Chapel stood on Station Road just past the infants school, facing the end of Tarry Hill. By 1904 there was a fourth chapel in the Fenhouses. Both of these are now disused.

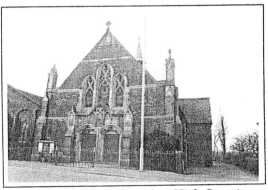

*14. Methodist Chapel in High Street
before demolition in 1986.*

CHAPTER FOUR

OLD FAMILIES OF SWINESHEAD

THERE WERE VARIOUS INFLUENTIAL FAMILIES who had a particular place in the history of Swineshead. One of the earliest of these was the Gresley family, members of which were at some time lords of the manor of Swineshead. The first Gresleys came over with William the Conqueror. The spelling of their name varies somewhat, appearing as Grelle, de Greslei, de Grelley, or most commonly as de Gresley.

In 1134 Robert de Gresley, of Manchester, owned a large area of marsh land in Lincolnshire on which he founded Swineshead Abbey. He was the son of Albert de Gresley, first Baron of Manchester.

When Robert de Gresley died his son, Albert, continued the patronage of the abbey. Albert married firstly Agnes, the daughter of Nicholas, Baron of Hatton; and secondly the daughter of Thomas Basset. Albert died in about 1175 and his son Robert, being only three years old, became the ward of William Basset, who was probably his uncle.

The Gresleys married into most of the influential families of the time. Robert, the son of Albert, married the daughter of Henry de Longchamps, who was the brother of William de Longchamps, Chancellor to Richard the Lionheart. Robert Gresley took part in the rebellion of the barons against King John and had his lands confiscated as a result, though he did regain them at a later date. His son Thomas, inherited his father's estate when his father died in 1230.

Thomas de Gresley is recorded as having paid 100 marks to be exempt from attending King Henry III in France in 1242, although he did accompany the King into Wales in 1258. Thomas was warden of the King's Forests and died about 1261. He had a son Peter, of whom little is known, who died before his father.

Peter's son, another Robert, was heir to his grandfather Thomas de Gresley, although at Thomas' death , like his great-grandfather before him, he was still under age. Robert married Hawyse the daughter and co-heir of John Burgh. Through this marriage Robert gained considerable lands. Hawyse was patron of the church in Swineshead in 1287, and a considerable benefactor of the village. In 1270 she gave money to construct a new dyke from Bicker Haven, flowing round the north side of Swineshead, and turning south-east at Sykemouth to run to the Simon Weir drain at Kirton Holme. Robert de Gresley died in 1281/2, holding lands in Swineshead and in possession of the advowson of the church. Hawyse de Gresley died in 1301/2.

Swineshead manor was at this time held by the Gresleys, of the Honour of Bolingbroke.

A word of explanation may be helpful here to clarify the forms of tenure in medieval times. Tenure involved holding land from a superior, thus making the occupier of the land a tenant. Barons and earls held land of the king and in return provided knight service in times of war, and aid in the form of money. This was known as free tenure as these services were considered to be given freely. This land could be passed on to succeeding generations. The barons in turn let portions of their land to lesser lords and minor nobility who would then owe them aid and service, also given freely. These lords and knights then let parcels of their land to their vassals in return for services of a more servile nature. The latter was known as unfree tenure. Free tenure, as well as knight service, might consist of free socage, serjeanty, frankalmoigne or divine service. (See glossary). The Gresleys held Swineshead manor from the Earl of Richmond, who held the Honour of Bolingbroke of the King.

Thomas de Gresley, the son of Robert and Hawyse, was made a Knight of the Bath in 1307, and summoned to Parliament in 1308-1311. Thomas died without issue and the barony of Gresley became extinct, but his estates, including Swineshead, passed to his sister Joanna who was the wife of John de la Warre.

John and Joanna de la Warre were the patrons of Swineshead

church for some years, Sir John from 1321 to 1340, and his wife from 1340 until her death. Sir John died in 1347, and Joanna died in 1354, holding the manors of Swineshead, Sixhills and Bloxham. (Six Hills is a small village near Market Rasen in the north of Lincolnshire: Bloxham is a village near Banbury in Oxfordshire.), The estates then passed to her grandson Sir Roger de la Warre, her only son John having died before 1347.

Sir Roger de la Warre, born 1329, was the son of John de la Warre and Margaret, daughter of Robert de Holland, another old family connected with Swineshead. Sir Roger married firstly Elizabeth, daughter of Adam Welles, and secondly Aliana (or Alianora), daughter of John, Baron Mowbray. Sir Roger was summoned to Parliament as Baron de la Warre in August 1362. He fought at Poitiers where he vied with Sir John Pelham for the prestige of taking the French King prisoner. Sir Roger died in August 1370 and is reputed to have been buried 'in the church of the Abbey of Swineshead'. In his will, made in 1368, he left a legacy to pay off the debts of his grandparents, Sir John and Lady Joan (Joanna) de la Warre, and also those of his mother, Lady Margaret. To his wife Alianora he left his 'vestments, books and other necessaries' belonging to his chapel. After all his legacies and debts were paid, the remainder of his goods were to be divided into three. A third was to go to his wife, a third to his children, and the remaining third was 'to be disposed of for the health of my soul'.

Sir Roger's son and heir John, the son of his first wife Elizabeth, succeeded. In 1383 Sir John de la Warre rented one salt pit and adjoining area to Thomas Jay of Swineshead for twenty years. This pit rendered 'seven midds of salt at St Barnabas and St John the Baptist'. Thomas Jay was required to build one new salt pit and Sir John was to have right of chase etc on the marsh. That same year he is recorded as renting to Ranulph Bolle a plot of land called the 'Duckspasture', for five years, for one hundred shillings. Sir John died unmarried in 1398/9 and was buried in the church of the Abbey of Swineshead. The estates then passed to his half-brother, Thomas de la Warre, who was the eldest son of his father's second wife Aliana.

Thomas de la Warre was a Clerk in Holy Orders and a Rector of the church of Manchester. He was also sometime Rector of New Sleaford. He preferred to be called Magister Thomas de la Warre and not Baron, and used that title when summoned to Parliament from 1399 to 1425. He was Rector of Swineshead three times in all, firstly in 1378-1382, and again in 1394-1400, when his brother Sir John de la Warre was patron of the church. He became rector again in 1422 when Thomas, Bishop of Durham, was the patron.

Some time around 1400 Thomas de la Warre gave 90 acres of meadow in Swineshead with appurtenances to the abbey. Four acres of this land were known as Maloweng. It has been suggested that this might have been an earlier name for the Manwarings, but this is extremely doubtful.

Thomas de la Warre died in 1426, in possession of the manor of Swineshead, plus the advowson of the abbey and church, and the chapel of St Adrians. He may have been buried in Swineshead church, where at one time a window showing his arms was inscribed *Orate pro bono statu Thome domine de la Warre* ('Pray for the good estate [standing] of Thomas Lord de la Warre').

Thomas had two younger brothers, Edward and John, but they both pre-deceased him, and when he died the estate again passed to a woman. Johanna, Thomas's sister, was the widow of Thomas, Lord West, and her second son Reginald, taking his uncle's name, became the sixth Baron de la Warre.

Reginald West, the sixth Baron, was summoned to Parliament as Lord la Warre in 1427. He married Margaret the daughter of Robert Thorley. In 1441 Reginald made a pilgrimage to the Holy Land. He died in 1454 seized of the manors of Sixhills, Bloxham and Swineshead, with the patronage of Swineshead Abbey and the chapel at Barthorpe. His son and heir was Sir Richard West, born about 1432.

Sir Richard West married, firstly, Catherine, daughter of Robert, Lord Hungerford. They had five sons, Thomas, John, Reginald, Edward and Richard, the latter becoming a Franciscan friar, and two daughters, Margaret and Margery. After Catherine died Sir Richard married Eleanor, daughter of Henry Percy, Earl of Northumberland. There was no issue from this marriage.

Thomas West, Sir Richard's eldest son and heir, born in 1456, was created a Knight of the Bath in 1494 and a Knight of the Garter in 1520. Thomas married firstly Elizabeth, sister and heir to Sir John Mortimer, by whom he had two sons and four daughters; and secondly, Eleanor daughter of Sir Roger Copley, by whom he had three sons and three daughters. Thomas West died in 1526, seized of the manors of Sixhills, Bloxham, and Swineshead.

Thomas West's eldest son William pre-deceased his father, and so the younger son Thomas then became heir. He married Elizabeth, daughter of Sir John Bonville, but died without issue in 1554.

What happened to the estates for the next few years is not clear. The Harleian Manuscript shows that in 1575, William, Lord de la Warre, held land in Swineshead and Wigtoft of the Honour of Bolingbroke formerly in the tenure of Robert de Grellie, by the service of two knights fees.

Rev Cragg wrote 'Eventually the Wests like their predecessors ended in the male line and early in the 17th century their possessions passed, again by marriage of the heiress, to the Pelhams.'

By 1624 the manor of Swineshead, (see over – p. 68) held of the Honour of Bolingbroke, was in the tenure of Herbert Pelham esq who died possessed of it on the 31st July of that year.

The Pelham family originated in Sussex. According to the Lincolnshire Pedigrees Vol 3, Herbert Pelham of Swineshead, who died in 1624, was the son of Herbert Pelham and Katharine Thacker of Sussex. He died on 13th July 1624 and was buried at Boston on the 20th July. However, the Ross MSS gives a different line of descent, stating that Herbert was the son of Sir William Pelham and Mary, the daughter of William Lord Sands.

Herbert Pelham's first wife was Penelope the daughter of Thomas, second Lord de la Warre. Herbert had four children with Penelope: Herbert, Edward, William and a daughter Penelope.

15. Swineshead Manor House, demolished in 1957 to make way for the (then) new Co-operative store.

Edward and William died without issue. Herbert, who was born in 1600, became an MP in Cromwell's Parliament in 1654.

Herbert (b. 1600), some time before 1674, had purchased land in New England, which was described as 'a fine estate near Boston' [Ross Mss.]. His second wife was Elizabeth (nee Bosvile) the widow of Roger Harlakenden of Massachusetts. Herbert's sister Penelope married Richard Bellingham, Governor of Massachusetts. Edward, Herbert's son by his second wife, inherited his father's lands in America. What happened to the manor of Swineshead is not clear. It may have passed to the eldest son, Waldegrave Pelham, baptised on 26th September 1627, and buried on 12th November 1699.

In 1658, William Lockton of Swineshead Abbey, in his will left to his son John the manor of Swineshead, which he says he purchased from Sir John Woldenholme. Sir John Woldenholme may have purchased the manor from the Pelhams.

Just how the manor of Swineshead (as distinct from the Abbey manor) passed down is unknown, but the old Swineshead manor house was still standing in the market place in the 1950's. It was at that time divided into shops, offices and living accomodation, but was demolished in 1957. On the site the Co-operative Society then built a new store, which later became a restaurant.

The Hollands of Estevening were another old family who lived in Swineshead for generations. One record states that the manor of Esteveninge, or Steveninge, was included in the land granted to Earl Alan by William the Conqueror. It was part of Donington Hundred and had previously belonged to Aldine the Saxon. Another record states that William the Conqueror granted the manor to Robert de Vici, and that it had previously belonged to Eilric.

The name Estevening has been spelt in many different ways, including East Evening, and may possibly have come from the word stover, or estover, meaning 'a tenant's right to collect wood'. The manor house of Estevening is said to have stood about 'half a mile from the parish church in the direction of Bicker', but there are no visible remains on the site today. At one time a packhorse road was reputed to cross over it.

The Hollands were tenants of the Manor of Estevening. Otho de Holland is the earliest recorded individual, living some time before the Norman Conquest. It is said that his son Sir Stephen de Holland, Knight, succeeded him in the reign of Edward the Confessor and was referred to as 'lord of Stephening alias Estoving Hall in Swineshead'.

Sir Stephen was succeeded in 1016 by his son Sir Ranulph de Holland. He held Stevenynge by half a knight's fee, and land in Schirebec (Skirbeck) of the Honour of Richmond.

His son, also called Ranulph married Cecily daughter of Sir John de Welle (or Welles). This Ranulph was also knighted. He and his wife had a son John.

Sir Ranulph's son, Sir John de Holland, succeeded his father. Just when is uncertain, but Sir John was living in 1169. He had two sons, Thomas who died without issue, and John who succeeded his father. This second Sir John was living in the time of Henry II (ie 1154-1189).

He was succeeded by his son, a third John, said to be living in the reign of King John (1199-1216). He in turn was followed by his son, yet another John, who was living in 1209.

Sir John de Holland (living 1209) had two sons, Sir Ralf de Holland, and Henry Holland from whom, according to Brooke, the Dukes of Exeter and Earls of Kent are descended, as also the Hollands of Denton, Lancashire. One of his great-grandsons, Sir Thomas Holland, living in 1353, was said to have married Joan Wake, the Fair Maid of Kent.

The descent of Ralf de Holland has been traced by George Holland, whilst the descent of Henry Holland has been traced by the historian Brooke.

George Holland, who was the secretary to Thomas Duke of Norfolk and the Clerk of the Council in the wars in France and Scotland, in 1563 claimed that members of the Holland family had been living at Estovening Hall 'without alteration or change eyther of house or name by XIII descent before the Conquest.'

He also said:

> The manor or lordship of Estovening never went from the Hollands since, and now my brother Thomas Hollande is heir and enjoyeth it. The same lordship hath by speciall charter very great priviledges and liberties viz. free chase and free warren, waiff, stray, felons goods and ought to pay no manner of tolle nor pays no rente but 5s to Castle Ward and a mark for his liberties whereby he may keep sessions within the lordship as Sir Thomas Holland my grandfather did who executed two felons at Drayton within his lordship arraigned and condemned at the said sessions.
>
> Edward Holland Earl of Kent who was killed beyond sea, was brought home and buried at Bourn Abbey about ten miles from Estevening Hall where I saw him lie entombed in

the midst of the quire with five or six of my ancestors entombed round about him and there did my grandfather in his latter days keep house and lies buried hard by him. None of the Hollands are buried in Swineshead church but only Sir John who lies flat in the Hollands quire there. The scripture of his burial being in french the date worn out.'

Geo Holland said in a further note:

' . . . my grandfather, a third Sir Thomas lies buried at Bourn Abbey. He had seven sons and made them all religious. Daly and Laurence to Ramsey, Daniel and George to Crowland, Richard to Walsingham and John to Barking (Barlings)'

According to George Holland, it is from Sir Ralf de Holland that the Hollands of Estevening are descended.

The line drawn by George Holland is sketchy and has been criticised by the Rev. Cragg, but is briefly given here:

1	Sir Ralf	= ? Held lands in Holbeach and Bicker in 1274
2	Sir John	= Margaret ... Issue 1 son and 2 daughters.
3	Sir John	= ?
4	Sir Thomas	= ?
5	Sir Thomas	= ?
6	Sir Thomas	= ?
7	Thomas	= ?
8	Sir Thomas	= Johanna dtr of Piers Tempest.
9	Sir Thomas	= . . . Sutton of Burton. Thomas died 1515.
10	Thomas	= Jane dtr of William Kareby(?)

The descent of Henry Holland according to Brooke is:

1	Henry	= ? Brother of Sir Ralf, 1 above.
2	Ingeramus	= ?
3	Robert alias John	= Maude dtr of Lord Zouch of Ashby.

Robert had a brother Henry. According to Bloomfield Henry was a baron in Parliament in 1314.

4	Robert	= ?. One daughter. Male line died

out. Of his brothers, Otho, Thomas, John, and Richard only John had male issue. This line became the Hollands of Devonshire.

Other records provide the following information:

At some time between 1178 and 1222, 'Ranulph' (Ralf) Holland gave the nuns of Sempringham 10 acres of arable land in Wyberton. He also made a gift to Swineshead Abbey in 1202 of two acres of land. Sir Ralf is said to have been buried at Swineshead Abbey in 1262.

In 1515, a Thomas Holland died 'seized of the manor of Estevening', leaving the estate to his son and heir, Thomas, who was aged thirty at the time of his father's death.

His son, also Thomas Holland, who was living in Swineshead in 1535, was sub-seneschal at the Abbey, just before the Dissolution.

The next record is of John Holland who died in 1689 leaving no issue. The manor of Estevening passed to his heir Thomas Holland esq of Silk Willoughby, who sold it to George Fairfax of Newton Kyme, in Yorkshire. Thomas Holland was buried on 15th March 1691 at Swineshead. He was probably the last male member of the Holland family to reside at Estevening.

In 1705 an Act of Parliament was passed for the sale of the manor of Estevening, which was then the property of the late Christopher Fairfax. It was to be sold to pay his debts and 'for the benefit of his children'. However, it seems that no sale took place at this time.

In 1841 it was sold by the trustees of Thomas Lodyngton Fairfax to Thomas Cooper of Swineshead, whose family still held it in 1854.

Nothing is left of the old manor house now, but a farm house standing not far from the suggested site, still bears the name of Stenning. Other families worthy of mention are the Woolmers and the Bolles.

The Woolmers married into most of the above families at some time. One of the earliest mentions of this family was in 1393 when Richard Woolmer was a legatee of Elizabeth la Warre in her will dated 12th October 1393. He was also an executor of the will of Sir John de la Warre, knight, dated 8th January 1397/8. Richard Woolmer had a son John Woolmer, said to be 'of Swineshead', who married the daughter of John Bell.

Their son, Richard Woolmer, in the latter part of the fifteenth century, married one of the daughters of Sir Thomas Holland of Stevening. Their grandson, Richard Woolmer was the supervisor of the will of Robert Bolle. Richard Woolmer's son, Gregory Woolmer of Swineshead, living in 1562, held the manors of Bloxholme and Thorpe, with appurtenances in Bracebridge.

Gregory Woolmer's eldest son, Sir Gregory, who was knighted at Whitehall in July 1603, married Elizabeth, daughter and heiress of William Fairfax. Samuel Woolmer, one of Gregory's younger sons, was mentioned in the will of Philip Lockton dated 1599, when he was left ten shillings in money. Samuel's daughter Mary married into the Bolle family. She had two children, Gregory Bolle and Francis Bolle, both of whom were legatees of their grandfather, Gregory Woolmer, in his will dated 2nd November 1575.

The Woolmer family lived in a mansion close by the site of the farm grange of the Abbey (Hardwick Grange), and there used to be an avenue of trees leading down to a swan pool there though there is no trace of either today. There were still Woolmers living in Swineshead as late as the eighteenth century, as Thomas Woolmer and his wife Susan had two children baptised there. Their son Thomas was baptised on 20th October 1700, and their daughter Elizabeth, was baptised on 20th July 1707. Unfortunately both these children died in infancy and the line seems to have died out.

The Bolles lived at Bolle Hall. In 1327 Ioland de Holland and Margaret his wife were to have custody of the lands and tenements lately belonging to William Bolle deceased. William Bolle's daughter and heiress, Cecilia, was under age, and the Hollands were to hold the lands until she came of age, for the rent of 8/6d per year. Cecilia Bolle died in 1362.

In 1391 William de Bolle petitioned the king for a licence 'to amortise the profits of the court of this place with certain lands and tenements in Swineshead, Gosberton, etc for a chaplain in the church of Wigtoft.'

In 1532, Robert Bolle of Swineshead made a will in which he left to his wife Johanna 'my capital messuage with appurt(enance)s and my pasture and an acre of hempland'. After her death it was to be sold and the money divided between their children Thomas, Robert and Isabell, who was married to Gilbert Daly of Boston.

He also left jointly to Thomas, and Isabell and Gylbert Daly, 'my tenement in Barthorpe, 1 pece of lande and 1 pingle lying in the chapel filde'. After other bequests leaving his household goods to his wife, £10 to his son Robert, and his third doublet to his brother Richard, the remainder of his estate was to be divided into three. One third of this was to go to 'the pore of Swyneshed', one third to 'the makyng the causey thorowe the town of Swyneshed', and the remainder to his executors, who were his wife, son Thomas and son-in-law Gylbert Daly. 'Richard Wolmer of Swyneshede, gentilman' was to have 40s for being supervisor of the will. This will was made on the 7th December 1532 and proved on the 23rd December of the same year.

The Bolles were among the families who served as Commissioners of Sewers. The Commissioners of Sewers sat at Boston and Spalding most frequently, but also at Bourne, Stamford, Sleaford, Market Deeping and Swineshead.

Another old family were the Coneys. The will of Richard Coney dated 26 March 1533, after requesting that he be buried in the churchyard at Swineshead, left to his son Robert a house 'lying in Denton and . . . land in Denton felde nowe in ye tenure of Richarde Massyngberde'. To his son George he left 'one house and appurt(enances) lying in Kyrton nygh the stone brigge'. To his youngest sons Thomas and Anthoney, who were both under sixteen, he left twenty shillings and a cow. His wife Johanna was to have 'the house I dwell in' for her lifetime and after her death it was to be sold and divided between Thomas and Anthoney. He also left to his son Robert 'all my toyllys of my profacion within my shoppe'. The executors were Johanna Coney, his wife, and Thomas Husle. The will was proved on 28th May 1533. (The nature of Richard Coney's 'profacion' is not given).

Other than those families named above there were the Dickensons, Pridgeons, Whitings, Hearts, Butlers, (all of whom were benefactors of the church and the poor), Varleys, Aubins, Gildentoes, Greenleafs (of Nut Hall), Tarrys (after whom Tarry Hill is named), Tennants, Masons, Gallicks and Hides.

74.

CHAPTER FIVE

THE VILLAGE ECONOMY

THE EARLIEST EVIDENCE OF ECONOMIC ACTIVITY is the Roman salt making referred to in chapter one, and at this early period there were probably fen dwellers existing by fishing and wild fowling. In 779 the *Anglo Saxon Chronicles* refer to tenant farms in Swineshead with pasture and meadow. The Domesday Book of 1086 refers to saltworks and meadow land in Drayton, as well as salthouses, a fishery and meadow land in Stenning.

In 1292/3 the abbot of Swineshead was granted a licence to hold a fair 'at the Chapel of St Saviour in Swineshead' by Edward I. This fair was to be held annually, on October 2nd. It was for the sale of cheese and onions, and was held on what is now known as Cheese Hill. This fair was still being held in 1896. Another fair, held annually on the first Thursday in June, was for the sale of cattle.

The Cistercian monks at the abbey made early attempts at drainage to improve the land and raised sheep, and in 1300 were exporting wool.

From the early twelfth century a weekly market was held in Swineshead every Thursday. In 1613 a Commission was appointed to suppress Swineshead market, as there were already thirty seven market towns in Lincolnshire and presumably the others feared competition. This move obviously failed as the market continued for a further two hundred years or so. It was in decline by 1800, and by 1830 to 1840 all that remained was a custom kept up by the farmers, of gathering on market day at one of the numerous public houses to discuss business and socialise.

It is likely that the local economy centred around mixed farming until the late eighteenth century, and further indications of mixed farming can be seen in the records of the Lockton family living at the abbey. In 1647 Elizabeth Lockton left half an acre of hemp land, eight cows, three steers, four calves, five sheep, some swine and poultry. John Lockton in his will of 1680, left orchards and pasture land.

Farming in Swineshead as late as the seventeenth and eighteenth centuries was still mainly pastoral, as the land was not generally suitable for arable farming at that time. Seasonal flooding may have been a problem, although early attempts at drainage, firstly by the monks and then by the wealthier landowners in the sixteenth and seventeenth centuries, had improved matters somewhat. (One early writer had referred to Drayton's 'foule and woosie Marsh').

In this pastoral economy a man's wealth was judged by the number of cattle he owned. In the early part of the sixteenth century a farmer with 25 head of cattle was considered wealthy, whereas a man with 5-17 animals was not. Thomas Rootes of Swineshead in about 1560 had 64 dairy cattle. Thomas Harrys, also of Swineshead, in November of 1591, still had 66 cattle left after selling his summer fattening stock.

In the mid-eighteenth century there was an outbreak of cattle disease in the area. This resulted in the deaths of hundreds of cattle. The dead beasts had to be buried, and special rates were levied to cover the cost. In the wapentake of Kirton a total of 6,628 beasts died. The villages which sufferered the most were Donington, where 1048 beast died, Gosberton, where 998 died and Swineshead, which lost 940 animals. The disease probably spread rapidly because so many different cattle were grazed together on the common land, including cattle from Scotland on their way to Smithfield market.

Soon afterwards common grazing land disappeared as Enclosure Acts came into force. Enclosure entailed the redistribution of the land in order to facilitate the development of better farming methods, such as were already being used on the continent. Local landowners (who saw personal benefit in enclosure) usually initiated proceedings to this end, as an Act of Parliament was necessary to authorise the division of the land in question. Before proceeding with enclosure each parish had to obtain its own Act. A meeting was held of the main landowners, and if it was decided that it would be desirable to enclose land in the parish then these landowners petitioned Parliament for leave to introduce a Bill for Enclosure. It then went through Parliament. Between 1760 and 1830 there were about three hundred such Acts of Parliament affecting parishes in Lincolnshire.

The people of Swineshead, in common with other villagers from the surrounding area, fattened their cattle on the Eight Hundred Fen, or Holland Fen as it is known today. Eleven parishes had a claim to common rights on the Eight Hundred Fen, but in 1767 an Act of Parliament was passed to divide and enclose this fen.

On the 26th August 1766, several gentlemen met at The Angel Inn at Sleaford to discuss the enclosure of The Eight Hundred Fen. It was resolved that a plan or survey of the fen with the number of houses, cottages and families with 'Right of Common' should be made, before petitioning for a Bill to be brought in. In October of that year a public meeting was held at Sleaford. Some of those present proposed to read a Bill for dividing and enclosing the fen, but the majority of those present objected as no survey had been produced. Despite the objections of the majority, and without any resolution being passed, a few proprietors signed the petition. The petition was sent to Parliament soon afterwards and was read for the first time on December 9th 1766.

On March 4th 1767, a petition against this enclosure was brought by Trinity College, Cambridge; Rev John Shaw, the Rector of Wyberton; and Zachary Chambers esq, Lord of the Manor of Swineshead. On March 6th the Bill was read for the second time. The petition was referred to the Parliamentary Committee.

On the 21st March, another petition against the Bill was made by Sir Charles Frederick, KB, sole owner of the land in Brothertoft, where there were fifty one cottages with Rights of Common on the Eight Hundred Fen. His petition was referred to the Committee.

Six days later Sir Gilbert Heathcote, Bart, along with various other people, also petitioned against the Bill, claiming that it was injurious to their interests. This petition was referred to the Committee.

77.

On the 29th April, the Committee reported that it had considered the several petitions. Some amendments were made to the Bill and it was sent to the House of Lords.

In the Lords Sir Gilbert Heathcote and Samuel Reynardson esq, both petitioned against it, but the Bill was passed on June 29th 1767.

These Acts were contained in substantial documents and included detailed provisions to be observed in implementing the enclosure. The Hautre Huntre Enclosure Act of 1767 covered 22,000 acres 'more or less'. It included the Eight Hundred or Holland Fen and other commonable places adjacent.

After initial allocations of land to Zachary Chambers, Lord of the Manor of Swineshead, and Charles Anderson Pelham, Lord of the Manor of Frampton, in compensation for their loss of the rights of soil and mines and quarries, the remaining land was divided between the eleven parishes which had 'Rights of Common' there.

These eleven parishes were Boston West, Skirbeck Quarter, Wyberton, Frampton, Kirton, Algarkirk, Fosdyke, Sutterton, Wigtoft, Swineshead and Brothertoft. Dogdyke was also included, not as a parish, but presumably as a hamlet which also enjoyed 'Rights of Common' on Holland Fen.

Zachary Chambers Esq, Lord of the Manor of Swineshead was alloted 120 acres in a piece called Brand End; Charles Anderson Pelham esq received 120 acres in a piece near Great Beets. After these allotments were made, the rest was divided between the eleven parishes in proportion to the number of houses in each. This land was to be the common fen of that township and subject to the same rights as the fen was before enclosure.

Each parish was responsible for fencing its portion of the fen. It was obvious that trouble was expected, as the penalty for destroying these fences was also set out in the document. First offenders were fined between £5-£20, or were sent to the House of Correction for up to three months; second offenders were fined £10-£40, or six to twelve months in the House of Correction; and third offenders were dealt with more harshly at Holland Quarter Sessions and could be transported for seven years.

The Act also provided for settling disputes, the setting out of private roads, ways, ditches etc although:

> '. . . nothing in this Act shall . . . impower the said Commissioners to alter or divert the Course of the present Turnpike Road leading from Boston to Swineshead . . .'

In 1774 the common land apportioned to Swineshead was eventually divided between individual villagers. The original document enumerating the various allotments, is deposited at the Lincolnshire Archives and extracts taken from it can be found in the Appendix.

The main beneficiaries of the enclosures were the lord of the manor, tithe owners who stood to gain increased rent, and the larger farmer. The smaller farmer was often forced to sell, because of the burden of his legal costs connected with enclosure and the cost of fencing in his land. The cottager suffered by the loss of common grazing land.

At the time the enclosure of Holland Fen was taking place, the associated unrest led to disturbances. The poor man had no other way of objecting to the enclosures, having no money to petition parliament, and so some took the law into their own hands.

There were several local incidents of rioting eventually leading to murder. One of the riot leaders was known as 'Gentleman' Smith. (See chapter 9).

Although enclosure was unpopular at the time, it eventually resulted in more efficient farming methods being developed, as the individual now had full control of his own land. Improved drainage and the use of new machinery assisted the process.

The basic farming economy of the district had to be serviced and so within the village there were blacksmiths for shoeing the horses, and making and repairing implements; millers for grinding the corn; the saddler and harness maker; wheelwrights to make and repair wagons; and also the normal domestic providers such as butchers, bakers, grocers, drapers and shoemakers.

In 1826 there was a spinning wheel maker in the village called Noah Thompson. There was also a glove making business owned by Joseph Powdrill, and William Johnson was a rope maker and flax dresser in the 1820's.

16. A typical sight in Swineshead earlier this century—potato pickers. Mr George Burrell is holding the horses' reins.

The first mail service was by post-boy on horseback, and later by mail coach. Incoming mail arrived at The Wheatsheaf Inn from where it could be collected. Similarly outgoing mail was despatched from the Wheatsheaf. In 1849 the postmistress was Mrs Mary Spring, and the mail was received and despatched at 9.30 am and 5.15 pm. In 1855 Richard Plant, the druggist, was the postmaster and receiver of the mail.

In 1882 William Eayr ran a grocers and 'fancy repository' in the corner of the market place next door to The Wheatsheaf. This was also the post office and the telephonic express delivery office where letters arrived daily at 7.15 am and were despatched at 6.00 pm on weekdays and 5.10 pm on Sundays. In 1922, Mr Albert Routen, who was also a grocer and draper, ran the post office.

A Stamford Mercury newspaper of 1859 reported that

17. Fruit pickers on William Gilding's farm, c. 1904.

Swineshead was in advance of its neighbouring villages as it had its own gasworks, but despite this there were no street lights in the village. The Swineshead Gas, Coal and Coke Company had been established in 1857 and was situated on Tarry Hill. In 1861 the company secretary was William Dolby Reddish.

In 1875, the same newspaper reported that the gasworks could not be made to pay by the present owners and so had been sold to Mr John Brown Jessop (who was also the landlord of The Griffin Inn). Mr Jessop intended to reduce the price of gas and had persuaded the church and chapels, which had stopped using gas, to once more begin to do so, and the streets were to be lit by gas again. Mr Jessop was considering another reduction in price very shortly in the hope that more of the inhabitants of Swineshead would be persuaded to use gas again, in preference to oil and candles.

Kelly's Directory of 1896 includes, other than farmers, the following professions in Swineshead: baker, brewers agent,

81.

18. Examples of packaging— goods sold in Swineshead around the
turn of the century. S. Steeper was the chemist in 1896 and
Holland's shop was trading in the early 1900s.

19. Shakelton's butcher's shop c. 1890, later bought by Christopher Dawson and demolished to build his new premises on the site (below). The Wheatsheaf Inn can be seen on the right and The Griffin Inn in the background.

20.

20. Mr Christopher Dawson standing outside his shop, early 1900s.

21. Eric Gadd's blacksmith's shop, with Eric Gadd in the centre standing outside it.

83.

dressmaker, carpenter & builder, butcher, bootmaker, carrier, ironmonger, baker & miller, blacksmith, market gardener, grocer & draper, shoemaker, wheelwright, potato dealer, harness maker, marine store dealer, monumental mason, cattle dealer, tailor, as well as keepers of beerhouses and public houses. In 1913 when Herbert Green, a journalist writing for a Boston newspaper, arrived in Swineshead by train, he walked the two miles to the village, remarking on the 'glorious landscape' either side of the road. On reaching the village he was delighted by the 'quaint old market place' and the gardens which he said were 'in the height of their glory'.

He went on to say that Swineshead parish stretched from Swineshead Bridge to within one and a half miles of Gosberton Church, and also bordered on the parish of Wigtoft. In another direction it reached Chapel Hill and was therefore a sprawling parish.

In 1913, in the corner of the market place, was William Holland's grocers and drapers stores. This was also a complete house furnishers and Mr Holland had a part of the old manor house as a storage room for some of his goods.

Green remarked that Swineshead was then a very prosperous village. Many of the young girls didn't go out to service as was customary, because it was more profitable for them to stay home

---

22. The Methodist Chapel on the right of the picture has been replaced by the fish and chip shop. The old cottages on the left of the photograph were occupied by Lal Fox, who worked as a miller at John Walter Smith's North End Mill; and Morris Atkinson who was a saddler. The man with the horse and cart could have been Len Smith, baker, who delivered in a cart like this.

23. High Street, from the village centre, as it appeared c. 1920. The thatched cottage on the left of the photograph was the local mole catcher's cottage, which later burnt down. The mole catcher was a Mr Holland and at the back of his cottage he generally had frames with moleskins stretched out to dry in the sun.

22. *South Street, Swineshead (and see opposite)*

23. *High Street, Swineshead (and see opposite)*

and help on the farm. The men were largely employed in agriculture. There were fifty seven farmers and eight market gardeners in and around Swineshead at that time.

Green also records that Swineshead was then a busy fruit growing area where Mr William Gilding was farming 170 acres. He grew gooseberries, raspberries, strawberries, and black and red currants. He also owned extensive apple orchards.

Mr John Brown had planted the orchards some years earlier, and Mr Goodwin, who took over from John Brown, later took William Gilding as his young partner. Joel Goodwin was probably Swineshead's first market gardener, and is credited with being the first in this area to grow spring cabbages and cauliflowers on a commercial basis.

After Goodwin's death, William Gilding continued to run the business although he didn't own the land, which was the property of Mrs Goodwin and the John Brown Trust. William Gilding also grew narcissus, and he had 50 acres down to broccoli, cabbage and lettuces. He was also an exporter of gooseberry bushes to America.

Some older residents may recall the village centre in the 1930's when Miss Eliza Jane Wright kept a general store and sweet shop in part of the old manor house in the Market Place; Routens had a shop in High Street which was later to become Metcalf's general store; Mr George Smithson was the chemist; Charles Mowbray had a cycle shop; Edward Mowbray, wheelwright, was soon to become Edward Mowbray, builder; Eric Gadd was a blacksmith on the main road opposite Jesse Scotney the harness maker; and Frank Horn was the local hairdresser.

As well as Holland's, and Wright's, in the old manor house were the solicitors Grocock & Staniland. Some parts of the manor house had been divided into living quarters, and some into shops.

On Cheese Hill there was a tinsmith known as 'Tinker' Dawson to distinguish him from Christopher Dawson the butcher, who had a shop on High Street just facing the market place. There were also two other butchers in the village, Len Grundy and Thomas Victor Rawlinson. For many generations important contributors to the economy of the area were the millers. Swineshead originally had at least five, and possibly six windmills, and in 1913 when Green visited the village, there were four windmills still operating.

The windmill at North End, which was a small tower mill, was built in 1821 on the site of a previous mill. A tower mill usually had a brick tower with four, five or seven floors in equal proportions. This one had three floors, two pairs of stones, a white painted ogee cap, a fantail, and four sails on a round brick tower. In 1932 one of the cog wheels broke. This had been part of the mechanism which turned the sails into the wind, and the breakage meant that the sails were then permanently jammed over the door. After that they could then only be used when the wind was in the one direction.

It is not clear who the miller was in 1821, but by 1849 a widow, Mary Henson, was running it with the help of two employees. She was only a young woman of 35, and had four daughters and two sons to support. She also had her sister and niece living with her.

24. North End Mill in the 1920s.

By 1865, Thomas Cartwright had taken over the mill at North End, and in 1891 Eli Dickenson was the miller, living there with his wife Charlotte and his daughter and two servants. He remained miller there until John Walter Smith purchased the mill in 1911. He ran it with the aid of Lal Fox, who was his miller, until Mr Smith's son joined the business some years later.

In 1983, John Walter Smith's son, Colin, sold the mill to David Bent, who is currently in the process of restoring it, using parts salvaged from other mills.

In 1911, at the same time as North End mill was sold to John Walter Smith, there was a bakehouse, dwelling house and grinding mill sold at the same auction. These were said to be bounded on the east by High Street, on the west and north by property of Mrs

Brighty, and on the south by property of Messrs Soulby, Sons & Winch.

Another mill, Houlder's Mill, was built in 1833 and was also a tower mill. In its latter days it was used with an engine and not sails. The mill was still operational in 1923. In 1963 it was all but demolished the only remains being just a stump of the tower, which itself was later demolished.

Drayton Mill stood not far from the supposed site of the Chapel of St Adrian. In 1849 it was in the ownership of Joseph Knight. By 1896 William Whittington, baker and miller had taken over. The mill at this time could be run by both wind and steam. In the 1913 White's Directory, William Whittington was described as a vegetable and potato merchant, farmer, miller and baker, with three addresses: Westholme, Drayton, and Sneinton Market, Nottinghamshire.

Drayton Mill was demolished in 1926. Mill Cottage, which stands near the site of Drayton mill, is possibly one of the oldest cottages in the village. (Later the mill site belonged to the Wests who were bakers in the village for some years).

There was a mill on Tarry Hill which was kept by Edward Stubley in 1849. By 1851, according to the census, it was kept by Edward Francis from Gosberton, and his wife Mary.

There had at one time

25. *Drayton Mill before demolition.*

been another mill in the village, according to the 1904 OS map which shows the site of a disused corn mill along Villa Lane. It stood opposite The Villa, and adjacent to a farm called The Ivy. There may also have been a mill on or near Mill Hill.

None of these mills is working today, and only one, North End mill, is still in existence. Corn is no longer ground locally, and wind power is a thing of the past, although the Maud Foster windmill in Boston has been restored to working order in recent years.

In agriculture the internal combustion engine is usually the motive power for today's machinery, and the combine harvester, the potato harvester, and the beet harvester are the machines of today. Since the days of William Gilding, fruit farming has largely disappeared, and the crops grown today are potatoes, sugar beet, cabbages, brussels, broccoli, and cereals, as well as salad crops under glass.

CHAPTER SIX

COMMUNICATIONS

THE FIRST BUILDERS OF ROADS in Lincolnshire were the Romans, who according to Stukeley (writing in 1724), built a road from Bolingbroke through Stickford and Sibsey, crossing the Hammond Beck by ferry and connecting Kirton and Gosberton to Donington and Horbling. This road, if it existed, would have passed within three miles of Swineshead, but Stukeley's claim has never been verified.

Roads in medieval times were little more than dirt tracks, dusty in summer or covered in mud and possibly flooded with water in the winter. There would be liberal amounts of horse manure and cow dung on the roadway, as cattle were taken to market along the same routes. Travelling therefore would not be an enjoyable nor a comfortable experience, as most people travelled on horseback or on foot, carriages being unknown except to the wealthy. Goods were transported by pack horse or by cart.

An undated map of Lincolnshire by Robert Morden, found in a directory at Lincolnshire Archives called simply 'Lincolnshire 1719', shows a road from Boston passing through Kirton and Swineshead and on to Donington, by-passing Bicker. The road then turned towards Sleaford, where it joined the road from Market Rasen and Lincoln. Another road ran from Boston to Kirton and Gosberton. No roads were shown running northwards from Boston.

The only other roads marked on this map ran from Grimsby, through Lincoln and on to Newark and Grantham, and another from Barton on Humber through Lincoln to join the one running from Sleaford to Market Deeping. No other roads were shown.

Throughout the years people of Swineshead made bequests in their wills for the upkeep of the roadways. Robert Bolle in his will dated 7th December 1532, left money for 'makying the causey thorowe the town of Swyneshed', and Thomas Overton, in 1533, left 13s 4d in his will, for repairs to the 'cawseys' in Swineshead.

Before he died in the latter part of the sixteenth century, John Butler gave land and property in Swineshead and Wigtoft in trust, for repairs to the 'Causeways belonging to the said parish of Swineshead'. This charity is still extant today. Butler's Charity was founded on 20th April 1570, when John Butler conveyed 'one Messuage, Barn, Stable, Outhouses, Garden, Yard, and Five Acres of Arable Land' to trustees, namely Thomas Hall junior and Thomas Hall senior, Henry Pridgin, Thomas Bullock, Anthony Hall, Richard Bull, Thomas Brotone, Gregory Sherwood, John Knight and William Maye. The income from this land was to be used for 'the mendinge and reparreinge of the highe Wayes leadinge to the p'ish Church of Swineshead . . . soe longe as the world shall endure . . . '

In an indenture dated 4th June 1641, the then trustees were John Harris, John Blisburye, Christopher Tarry and John Ereswell, said to be the 'ffoure surviveinge ffeoffyes of John Butler'. In this document the property was said to be situated 'betweene the lands of the Lord de Lawarre & lands late George Heyseiles towards the South & the lands of John Saltonstall gent & Sr Sutton Cony knight towards the North & abutts a Certayne place called the Towne Feild towards the East, & upon the Kings highe Way towards the West'.

From the middle of the sixteenth century each parish was responsible for maintaining the roads running through it. By a statute of 1555, the parishioners were obliged to spend four days a year working on the roads under the supervision of surveyors appointed by the parish churchwarden. In 1563 the number of days required was increased to six. In winter the roughly constructed roads were muddy, wet, or icy; in spring they could be flooded; and in summer they were dry and dusty. Trade was hampered by a lack of good roads, even though many goods travelled by sea or river. Eventually the increasing volume of traffic, shortage of money, and the lack of enthusiasm on the part of the villagers who were required to supply the free labour, created so many problems that this system broke down. All these factors contributed to the coming of the Turnpike Trusts.

Turnpike Trusts had the power to levy a toll on the users of their particular stretch of roadway, although no tolls were levied on the mail coaches, the military, or people who were on their way to church on Sundays. The money thus levied was then used to repair the road surface.

The first road in England to be turnpiked was a stretch of the Great North Road between Wadesmill in Hertfordshire and Stilton in Huntingdonshire. This was in 1663. The first Lincolnshire roads to be turnpiked were also stretches of the Great North Road, but this was not until 1726 and again in 1739.

In the early part of the eighteenth century the roadways around Swineshead were still rather primitive. In the winter of 1750 it was still generally considered prudent to hire a guide when travelling from Swineshead to Sleaford, as in the wet weather the roads were treacherous. At this time there were more animals than people on the roads, cattle being driven to London to the Smithfield Market and geese, with their tarred feet, also being driven from place to place to be sold.

In 1758 the Donington Trust was formed. It was responsible for the ten miles of road from Donington Bridge End to Boston which ran through Swineshead. To establish a turnpike system the parish authorities had to apply to the government for an Act of Parliament to create a trust for each particular stretch of roadway. When this Act was passed it lasted for twenty one years. At the end of this time the Act had to be renewed for a further twenty one years. In 1758, when the Act was passed to turnpike the road through Swineshead, the management of Butler's Charity was taken away from the trustees. This remained so until 1822, when Swineshead Parish regained control of the charity and trustees were once again appointed. This charity then maintained the pavements, and in later years provided street lighting. Today it supports sporting organisations, by providing land for the Football and Bowls Clubs rent free.

The section of road from Boston to Swineshead was turnpiked in 1764. This road reached Swineshead at the north end of the village. The turnpike branched here to join the Lincoln Heath

93.

Trust. A branch road was also built at this time to Langrick Ferry and on to Holland Fen, where there was a gravel pit which supplied material to repair and build the roads. A new Trust, formed in 1826, also connected the road from Fosdyke Bridge to the Boston/Donington road to Swineshead.

Even after the coming of the turnpike road winter travel could still be difficult. According to Pishey Thompson 'The whole of the land between Brothertoft and Boston was frequently overflowed during the winter season. The turnpike road from Boston to Swineshead and the intersecting roads leading to the adjacent villages were often covered with a considerable depth of water.' He goes on to say that the country people, in such times, brought their goods to Boston by boat when it was possible to reach Rosegarth Street and sometimes the White Horse Inn at the top of West Street. It was only after the enclosure of Holland Fen in 1768 - 1774, and the associated drainage, that this situation improved.

Turnpikes took their name from the barrier across the road, which was in the form of a pivoted bar similar to the modern railway barrier. The 1851 census for Swineshead shows William Newton, toll collector at Linger House Toll Gate. This revolution in the English road system meant that roads were improved and travel and trade made easier. The road improvements in the eighteenth century also benefited the mail, which was originally carried by post boys on horseback, but from 1784 was able to be delivered by coach. In that year the first Royal Mail Coach ran between London and Bath. Mail coaches eventually carried passengers too, enabling people to travel more easily. The coaching era lasted over 50 years, but when the railway arrived coaching gradually declined.

Local carriers, too, would have appreciated the new turnpike. The ordinary person wishing to go to Boston and not wanting to walk the seven or so miles from Swineshead could pay the carrier for a ride on his cart, for which the carrier would charge a penny a mile. The carrier would also take goods to market for farmers by arrangement and deliver them to the local shops, or sometimes he would purchase goods such as eggs or chickens to sell himself at a small profit. For a small fee he would even purchase goods for the farmer's wife such as tea, medicines, cottons and other small items.

In 1826 there were two carriers who departed for Boston every Wednesday and Saturday at 6am, John Allbones and a Mr Cooke. This may have been William Cooke who was carrier in Swineshead until at least 1856. Presumably his son had taken over by 1861, when there were three carriers from Swineshead to Boston each market day; Samuel Cooke, William Lister, and Henry Lowe. Samuel Cooke was still in business in 1896, but by 1913 the carrier was William Wade and in 1922, White's Directory listed only one carrier, Frederick Trevor.

Another mode of travel was by water. Joseph Kinners owned a packet which sailed from the Fortyfoot Bridge to Boston, Lincoln, and even as far as Yorkshire. There were no regular times of

26. High Street, Swineshead, c. 1905
[Photograph courtesy Lincoln Library]

departure, so presumably this was a somewhat unreliable method of travel. It was also a cheap way to travel but a slow one, as less than six miles per hour was achieved and there were constant delays to take goods on board.

Communications were further improved with the advent of the railway, which came to serve Swineshead in 1859 when the Sleaford to Boston line was opened. It became quicker to go to Boston by train than by road or water. The train was a much

27. A carriage licence. Mr Gibbons was a smallholder at Brand End in the 1920s. (Not exactly a 'tax disc' – but not dissimilar in function.)

quicker and more comfortable mode of travel and was not expensive, with it's third class rate being competitive with the local road carrier. The railways charged 2d per mile first class; a penny ha'penny per mile second class; and only one penny a mile third class. The line from Swineshead to Boston was single track initially, but by 1881 it had been made into a double line. (Following the Beeching report and the reorganisation of the railways in the 1960's, the line reverted to single track in places).

Although it stood two miles away from the village, Swineshead station was a busy one. It had its own coal yard, and nearby were a blacksmith's shop, two public houses, and a few cottages.

Now that the farmers had a quick and cheap method of transport, they moved their cattle by rail. One landowner even had his own narrow gauge railway running along Brown's Drove, to carry goods to and from the station. This proved uneconomical

28. Station Street as it used to be—traffic free.

however, as it couldn't carry large loads, and it soon fell into disuse.

In 1881 the station master was George Tuckerman from Ashburton, in Devon, who was married with six children, all of whom were born in different places. Only the baby aged nine months was born in Swineshead. By 1891 the station master was William Geeson, from Leicestershire, who was married with a family of six children, born in three different places; and in 1896 Robert Daws had taken over the job.

It was not until the last few years of the nineteenth century that a new form of travel arrived – the bicycle. In the early part of the twentieth century the bicycle became a common sight providing a cheap means of travel for people to visit local towns. Contrast the difference, in time and effort, between walking and cycling to Boston from Swineshead. The cycle probably contributed more than anything else in breaking down the relative isolation of rural communities before the motor car came into widespread use after the Second World War.

CHAPTER SEVEN

THE POOR, THE POOR LAW, AND THE WORKHOUSE

FROM THE SIXTH CENTURY ONWARDS the relief of poverty was assumed by the Church. One third of the church tithes was supposed to be allocated to the poor, but this system seems to have ceased by the 1100s. It was left to the monasteries, abbeys, and convents to offer food at the gate to any poor people who came, and sometimes they would offer lodging to destitute travellers and occasionally care for orphans.

Individuals would often leave money in their will for the poor of the locality, as to give to the poor was considered to be a way of ensuring one's salvation. For example, Roger de la Warre, in 1360, left £100 for the poor, to be distributed at half a mark each for as many poor people as his executors saw fit. Philip Lockton, gent, in his will dated 10th April 1599, left £3 to buy coal when it was at its cheapest, which was to be sold to the poor in the winter at the cheap rate, forever.

But it wasn't only the rich who left money to the poor. Others less wealthy, such as William Benlay of Swineshead, in his will dated 13th November 1531, left 'To the fatherles chyldren at St Catheryns iiijd' (fourpence). St Catheryn's was an orphanage in Lincoln run by nuns.

In the fourteenth and fifteenth centuries the various guilds gave alms to their members who fell on hard times, made provision for widows and orphans and sometimes found lodgings for strangers and homeless people.

The parish raised money for its poor by taking collections in church on Sundays. It also made use of the 'Parish Stock'. The Parish Stock, or Church Stock, was in some cases a flock of sheep or herd of cattle, used to raise money for parish purposes. The milk from the cows might be distributed to the poor and needy, and money from the sale of stock was used for the relief of poverty. These animals were sometimes gifts or bequests left by parishioners in their will, and flocks such as these continued in some places until the seventeenth century, although no such 'stock' is recorded at Swineshead.

From 1536 each parish was responsible for its own poor and was unwilling to accept responsibility for those belonging to any other parish. In 1662 the Law of Settlement and Removal was passed to prevent vagrancy and enable the parish overseers to return any poor family or individual trying to settle in the village to their original parish. A certificate was made out and the unfortunate individual or family was dispatched promptly to their place of origin, before they could become a burden on the parish. This situation lasted for the next 130 years. The following is the Removal Order for John Brewster and his wife of Swineshead, who were being removed from Frampton:

> To the Churchwardens & Overseers of the Poor in the Parish of *fframpton* in the said pash and County and to the Churchwardens and Overseers of the Poor of the Parish of Swineshead in the *said pash and County*.
>
> Whereas complaint hath been made by you the Churchwardens and Overseers of the Poor of the said Parish of *fframpton* unto us whose Hands and Seals are hereunto set, two of His Majesty's Justices of the Peace (Quorum unus) for the *pash & County* aforesaid, That *John Brewster & his wife* lately intruded *themselves* into your said Parish of *fframpton* there to Inhabit as Parishioners contrary to the Laws relating to the Settlement of the Poor, and are there likely to become Chargeable, if not timely prevented: And whereas, upon due Examination and Equiry (sic) made into the Premises, *on the Oath of this said John Brewster* it appears unto Us, and We accordingly Adjudge, That the said *John Brewster & his wife* are likely to become Chargeable unto the said Parish of *fframpton* & that the last Legal Place of Settlement of the said *John Brewster* was in the said Parish of *Swineshead.*
>
> These are therefore, in His Majesty's name, to Order and Require you the said Churchwardens and Overseers of the Poor of the Parish of *fframpton* aforesaid, that you, or some of

you, do forthwith Remove and Convey the said *John Brewster & his wife* from your said Parish of *fframpton* to the said Parish of *Swineshead* and *them* deliver to the Churchwardens and Overseers of the Poor there, or some or one of them, together with this our Warrent or Order, or a true Copy hereof, whereby they are likewise Required, in His Majesty's name, and by Virtue of the Statutes in such Case made, forthwith to receive the said *John Brewster & his wife* into their said *parish of Swineshead* and provide for them as their own Parishioner.

Given under the Hands and Seals, the *22nd Day of November* Anno Regni *(dai 1171 Georgii sier Regni)* nunc Magnae Britanniae, Etc *primo* Annoq; Dom' 1727

Lincoln
Holland.
Richard Gilbert.

Another record acknowledging responsibility by the Algarkirk Overseers for the family of John Gamble, who were living in Swineshead reads:

'Lincoln Holland
Algerkirk

September the 23: Whereas John Gamble with His wife and childe Inhabitants of Algerkirk afore said is or intended to come to be Inhabitants of the towne of Swineshead in the parts & county aforesaid: therefore if the said John Gamble his wife or Childe or any of them shall at any time hereafter become chargeable to the said towne and parrish of Swinehead aforesaid: according to An Act of Parlement in that Case made and provided we the Minister Churchwardens Overseers of the Poor and other inhabitants of the towne & Parrish of Algerkirk aforesaid doe promis and Ingage unto the Minister Churchwardens and Overseers of the Poor & other Inhabitants of the towne of Swineshead aforesaid to receive the said John Gamble His wife & Childe or any of them back to our sd towne and Parrish of Algerkirk aforesd and shall & will take care and provide for the said John Gamble his Wife and Childe or any of them as our owne poor soe that they or any of them shall not at any time hereafter become chargable to your towne and Parrish of Swineshead aforesaid In witness whereof we the Minister Churchwardens Overseers of the Poor set our hands and seales the day and year first above written.'

The Overseers of the Poor also had responsibility for placing poor children of working age in positions where they would learn a trade. A typical apprenticeship Indenture was that of John Clarke, a pauper child who was apprenticed as a servant to Thomas Smith of Swineshead in 1698.

'This Indenture made the Eighth Day of March in the Eleventh Year of the Reign of our Sovereign Lord King William — — — by the Grace of God of England, Scotland, France and Ireland, Defender of the Faith, &c. Annoque Dom. 1698 Witnesseth, That Thomas Jessop and John Sharpe Churchwardens of the Parish of Swineshead in the pt of Holland County of Lincoln And Thomas Ellis gen Jeremiah Hobson Overseers of the Poor of the said Parish, by and with the Consent of his Majesties Justicies of the Peace of the said County whose Names are hereunto subscribed, have put and placed and by these Presents do put and place John Clarke a poor Child of the said Parish, Apprentice to Thomas Smith gen of Swineshead, afore sd with him to dwell and serve from the Day and the Date of these Presents, until the said Apprentice shall accomplish his full Age of four and twenty years according to the Statute in that case made provided: During all which Term, the said Apprentice his said Master faithfully shall serve, in all lawfull Businesses according to his Power, Wit, and Ability; and honestly, orderly, and obediently in all things demean and behave himself towards his said Master and all his during the said term. And the said Thomas Smith doth Covenant and grant for himself his Executors and Administrators, to and with the said Church-Wardens and Overseers, and every of them, their and every of their Executors and Administrators, and their and every of their Successors for the time being, by these Presents, That he the said Thomas Smith (John Clarke) the said Apprentice, in the Art of Husbandry shall teach and instruct And shall and will during all the Term afore said find, provide, and allow unto the said Apprentice competant and sufficient Meat, Drink, Apparel, Lodging, Washing, and all other Things necessary and fit for an Apprentice. And Also shall and will so provide for the said apprentice, that he be not any way a Charge to the said Parish, or to the Parishioners of the same; but of and from all Charge shall and will save the said Parish and Parishioners harmless and indemnfied during the said Term. And at the end of the said Term shall and will make, provide, allow and deliver unto the said Apprentice double Apparel of all sorts, good and new; that is to say, a good new Suit for the Holy-days, and another for the Working-days. In Witness whereof the Parties abovesaid to these present Indentures interchangeable have put their Hands and Seals the Day and year above-written.'

This document was then signed by Thomas Smith, Thomas Ellis, Thomas Jessop and Jeremiah Hobson, and three other witnesses.

The parish also took care of children born to unmarried women, and if the father was known he had to sign a Bastardy Bond accepting responsibility for his child, as in the case of Thomas Hare in 1735:

'Know All Men by these presents that I Thomas Hare of Swineshead in the county of Lincoln Husbandman am held and firmly bound unto William Brown of the same place Churchwarden and Herbert Ingram and Thomas Brown of the same place Overseers of the Poor in the sum of fifty Pounds of Good and Lawfull mony of Great Britain to be paid to the said William Brown Herbert Ingram and Thomas Brown or their certain Attorney or Successors to which payments well and truly to be made I bind myself my heirs Executors and Administrators firmly by these presents sealed with my seal dated the fourteenth day of April in the Eighth Year of the Reign of our Sovereign Lord George the Second by the grace of God of Great Brittain ffrance and Ireland King Defender of the faith and so forth and in the year of Our Lord one thousand seven hundred and thirty five.

The Condition of this Obligation is such that whereas one Jane Ryley of late been delivered of a Man child within the Parish of Swineshead aforesaid to the which child the above bounded Thomas Hare doth acknowledge himself to be the father if therefore the said Thomas Hare his heirs Executors or Assigns or every or any one of them do from time to time and at all times hereafter full and clearly acquit discharge and save harmless as well the within named William Brown Churchwarden Herbert Ingram and Thomas Brown Overseers of the Poor of Swineshead aforesaid and their successors for the time being and every of Thomas also all the Inhabitants and Parishioners of the said Parish which now are or hereafter shall be for the time being of and from all & manner of costs charges and expenses whatsoever which shall or may in any mannerrof wise at any time hereafter arise for or by reason or means of the berth and duration and bringing up of the said Child that the this obligation to be Void or else to be and remain in full force and Virtue.

Sealed and deliverd (being
first duly stamped) in the
presence of
Christopher Bree   the mark of
Wm Saywell   Thomas Hare

In the sixteenth to eighteenth centuries each parish had a poor-house. The parish poor-house was often a cottage or cottages where free lodgings could be had by the poor of the parish. They could also be a temporary shelter for vagrants and sometimes a place for the disabled and sick. They were often dirty and disorderly places, and were the forerunner of the workhouses. There was generally no supervision in these poor houses, and the inmates were responsible for feeding themselves. By the nineteenth century the workhouses had taken over from the poor-houses in most areas.

In 1815 there were more than 4000 workhouses in the country, containing approximately 100,000 residents. The inmates were generally put to work spinning, weaving, knitting, making sacks or fishing nets and even cultivating the land.

As well as the poor, others detained in the workhouse were lunatics and vagrants. Dangerous lunatics could not be detained in a workhouse for more than 14 days, according to the Poor Law Amendment Act, but milder cases were kept there longer. Able bodied vagrants could get food and a nights lodging for six hours work. Workers attracted by industry in the towns to seek employment there, and discharged soldiers were others who might be classed as vagrants.

There was a workhouse in Swineshead on Tarry Hill. Although

29. *Tarry Hill, showing Heart's cottages (behind the pedestrian).*
These cottages formed the original workhouse.
[Photograph courtesy Lincoln Library. Photograph taken c. 1905]

it is unclear when it was built, it was there in the late 1700s, as one writer referring to the catering standards of workhouses, stated that 'towards the end of the 18th century at Swineshead (workhouse) they were using waterpottage, made from water, oatmeal and onions.'

In the early part of the nineteenth century, the Master of this workhouse was Joseph Cope. The parish registers of St. Mary give various entries of bastard children being baptised whose single mothers were at that time living in the workhouse.

Between 1814 and 1824 there were twenty baptisms of infants born in the workhouse, but not all of them lived. Harriet, born on November 30th 1815 to Hannah Spittlehouse, was baptised the next day, and buried on January 20th 1816. Mary Woods, born April 24th 1816 to Elizabeth Woods, spinster, was baptised two days later, but was buried on May 9th of that year. Another young woman, Elizabeth Auckland, gave birth to a son in the workhouse on 23rd August 1815. She named him John Pearson Auckland; he was baptised on the 24th August, and died on the 27th.

On 29th December 1818, Mary Stretton, spinster, gave birth to a son, Richard Taylor Stretton. The child lived, but Mary, who was twenty-five years old, died on 16th March the following year, leaving her three month old infant son to be raised in the workhouse.

They weren't always single mothers, sometimes a married couple would be there long enough to have a family. A labourer, John Chamberlain and his wife Mary, had two children in the workhouse; William, baptised on 2nd April 1819, and Frederick, baptised on 1st February 1821. Unfortunately Frederick died on 14th February when only thirteen days old, and was swiftly followed by his mother Mary, who died eleven days later. Mary Chamberlain was only twenty-six years old.

Others who died in the workhouse between 1815 and 1821, and were buried from there were Sarah Filer, who was only aged seven; Thomas Waters, aged twenty-three; James Duffy, an Irishman aged twenty-six; Richard Barnwell alias Fisher, aged sixty-three; and Ann Tall aged seventy-six. (For a list of workhouse baptisms and burials see appendix).

In 1834 The Poor Law Amendment Act which came into force was an attempt to cut down on expenditure. It abolished outdoor relief for the able bodied who would now have to enter the workhouse in order to receive any benefits. As life in the workhouse was very harsh this deterred all but the most needy.

The discipline was harsh, the diet poor, and a man and his wife could be split up and forced to live in separate parts of the building.

In 1834, the 15,500 parishes throughout the country were arranged into 643 groups called Unions. Each Union was governed by an elected Board of Guardians, who were mostly property owners, such as gentlemen, farmers, butchers, druggists, and perhaps one of the local vicars. Boston Union was formed on 22nd of September 1836, and from this date Swineshead was part of this union. This was probably when the workhouse on Tarry Hill was closed, as the poor of Swineshead were then sent to the Boston workhouse, although there are no entries for baptisms or burials in Swineshead registers after 1824 that are specified as being from the workhouse.

This new system enabled the average expenditure on poor relief per head of population to be reduced by over 30% in the first three years. Expenditure on the poor had increased from £2 million in 1794 to £8 million in 1818. It was still around £7 million in 1834 when this Act was passed. By this Act, all relief to the able bodied was refused or, if given, the conditions were such that they deterred all but the most desperate from accepting them.

Each union had its own workhouse, and most unions built a new one. Each of these workhouses was to be managed by an unpaid, elected Board of Guardians, who employed the staff who ran the workhouse, ie matron, schoolmaster, receiving officers etc. The Guardians usually held meetings every fortnight to discuss the running of the workhouse.

Workhouse Masters and Matrons were generally married couples. No special qualifications were required for the job, which was not an easy one, as the workhouse was a mixture of school, asylum, hospital and workshop.

No records of the old Swineshead workhouse on Tarry Hill, which was used before the 1834 Poor Law Amendment Act, and possibly up until 1837, have been traced.

The Boston Union Workhouse opened in 1837 and the Admission and Discharge record book for 1838-9 contains the following entries relating to Swineshead people:

Name	Born	Admitted	'Discharged
Sarah Falkner	1830	Old inmate	29th Sept. Leave for 14 days.
Esther Potter	1828	Old inmate	
Rebecca Pell	1819	Old inmate	
Charles Pell	1838	Old inmate	
Susan Wilson	1791	Old inmate	29th June at her own request.
Jas Wilson	1826	Old inmate	With his mother.
Benjn Wanty	1801	Old inmate	
Susan Wanty	1798	Old inmate	
Jacob Wanty	1824	Old inmate	14th Aug. Gone on trial to M Martin. £1.15s per ann if he suits.
Wm Wanty	1827	Old inmate	
Ann Wanty	1826	Old inmate	18th July. Gone on trial for 14 days to Miss Ashton, Penn St.
Samuel Wanty	1830	Old inmate	
Jane Wanty	1833	Old inmate	
Rebecca Wanty	1837	Old inmate	
Eliza Yates	1830	Old inmate	24th April 1839. Taken by her father.
Hannnah Roberts	1790	26th July	1st Sept at her own request. Calling none. Single. Partially disabled. Pregnant - has had 3 illegitimate children.
Charles Roberts		—	With his mother
Richard Sutton	1786	2nd August.	18th Aug. At his own request. Shoemaker married.
Rebecca Sutton	1792	2nd August	With her husband.
Henry Sutton	1832	2nd August	With parents.
Zachariah Sutton	1830	2nd August	With parents.
Harriet Sutton	1835	2nd August	With parents.

These entries show that the workhouse was not only a place where the destitute elderly and infirm ended their days, or where passing vagrants were lodged, but was also a temporary haven for the single pregnant mother, and the temporarily jobless or homeless person.

Another record, the Census of 1891, shows that in Boston Union Workhouse there were nine people who came from Swineshead. Elizabeth Amelia Favell, aged fifty-three, the widow of an agricultural labourer; Joseph Rodgers, aged forty-five, was single and was a discharged soldier; George Smith, a seventy four year old widower and a retired agricultural labourer; Robert Jackson a single man of seventy six was another agricultural labourer; Daniel Wilson, widower, aged seventy four, had been a bricklayer; Sarah Stubley, a single retired charwoman and field worker, aged seventy three; Charlotte Woodward, a single thirty year old domestic servant; and two more agricultural labourers, William Stubley, married and aged sixty nine, and William Botheway, single and aged fifty nine.

Workhouse children were entered into an apprenticeship at an early age to rid the parish of the responsibility for their keep.

Over the years Swineshead had many benefactors who left money, land and/or property for the poor of the village.

In 1576, Henry Prigeon endowed eight acres of land in Milne Green, three acres of pasture in Quadring Eaudyke and ten and a half acres of land in Swineshead, to be used for the benefit of the poor.

Other similar bequests were: 1532, Robert Bolle left a third of the 'remainder' of his estate to the poor of Swineshead; 1585, John Lockton left £15 to the poor of the village; 1593, Robert Lockton left 6d each for eighty poor people; 1611, Sir John Lockton left £6.13.4d to the poor of Swineshead and Wigtoft; 1634, Dame Frances Lockton left £5 to the poor of Swineshead and 40s to the poor of Wigtoft.

Another benefactor, Thomas Dickonson, in his will dated 9th March 1674, gave to the vicar of Swineshead and his successors, one and a half acres next to Gallow Field, near Stump Cross, the money from which was to pay for two sermons to be preached annually on 21st December and 'the next Lord's Day after Easter.' He also left one cottage and yard with appurtenances and half an acre of pasture land, the rent of which was to be given to the poor on St Thomas' day each year.

An interesting document dated 9th July 1713 survives in the Poor Law records. This is an agreement for the construction of some new houses on land given by 'Mr Thomas Dickonson dec'd'. The document states that:

> 'William Browne [carpenter] . . . doth covenant article and agree to and with the said Samuell Smith and William Talkes [Overseers of the Poor] . . . that he the said William Browne his Executors or Administrators shall and will at his and theire proper costs and charges on or before the Twenty Ninth day of September next ensuing the date hereof for and in consideration of the sume of Threescore Pounds of lawful money of Great Brittaine to be paid to the sd William Browne . . . upon the day hereafter expressed provide good and sufficient oake and other materialls and new build frame and make Eight new houses or new Roomes all containing in length One Hundred and Twenty foot ffour whereof to be built upon the most convenient place of the ground given by Mr Thomas Dickonson decsd to the Poor of Swineshead lying in Swineshead aforesaid near the Queen's highway of the West as shall be appointed by the said Overseers. . . . And the other ffour new houses or Roomes to be built in some convenient place within the Parish of Swineshead afore said as shall be appointed by the sd Overseers with the consent of the Parishioners of Swineshead . . . '

The document goes on to give specific details stating that the:

> 'Eight new houses or Roomes [were] to be laid out as to the length thereof according to the discretion of the sd Overseers and the said severall houses or Roomes to be Twelve ffoot and an halfe wide from out to out with good and sufficient oake side plates maine Posts prick posts armes braces balkes beames and all other manner of Woodworks whereby to make the same good and sufficient brandrith the

said Posts on the lower part of the sd ground and all other posts to be answerable to the same and to be double outertraced and alsoe good and sufficient buncupples oake sparrs sidewavers and rigtrees answerable to the roofes and pin and fix the same too and doe all things else soe as to make the same good and sufficient oake roofes and to groundsole all the said houses or roomes with good brick a foot high above the ground and to build and make ffour good and sufficient double Chimneys therein of a neccessary and answerable length and wideness and the hearths therein to be made with brick a yard long and a foot and a halfe wide and the severall huds(?) to be answerable to the same and build the sd Chimneys with brick as high as the balkes and to make frame and put up good and sufficient oake Mantletrees to every Chimney of a due length and to build the Chimneys with brick three foot and a halfe above the brandriths and shall provide good splints and make good walling earth for the splinting and daubing of the sd Walls for the said houses or roomes as well with inside as without and alsoe all the Partition Walls as high as the beames and alsoe the Chimneys where the same are not to be brickt and well and sufficiently splint and daube the same and shall build and make ffour good and sufficient Ovens in the sd houses or roomes where the Overseers shall think most convenient and well sole the same sole the same each oven to be large enough to bake six pecks of Moulter And shall and will provide frame and make light Oake fframes and Windows stantialls and glass each Window to have four foot glass and to lead sander and band the same with lead sufficiently and put up one in each roome. And to provide a good reed thatch thread and thatch the same houses or roomes and well and sufficiently ridge the same with earth and shall provide good dailes and oake and make Eight good dores & durnes and Thresholds for the same & dore for every roome and good Iron hookes & bands for the hanging of the sd dores And alsoe provide set and fix to each dore a good & sufficient lock and Key & all other apptinnces and to provide nailes and other materialls and other Workmanship for the making sufficient and compleat the sd houses or roomes.'

For all this work William Browne was to be paid the: 'sume of Threescore Pounds on or upon the Twenty Eight day of May next ensuing . . . ' This document was signed by, among others, Marke Dickonson, Robert Burkley, George Pell, William Robinson, and Samuel Smith, also Stephen Carness and William Talkes who both made their marks.

In 1699 William Heart of Cottingham in Northamptonshire, gave to the poor of Swineshead one windmill and two cottages, a piece of ground near Tarry Hill, and five roods of land in Town Field, the rents of which were to be distributed to the poor by the Churchwardens on the first Sunday after St Martins and on Whit Sunday, for ever.

John Dickonson in his will dated 27th January 1719, left three acres of land to the vicar and his successors forever, to preach a charity sermon yearly on the anniversary of his death.

William Whiting, in his will dated 19th March 1726, left to the poor of Swineshead a messuage and tenement with half an acre. The rent of this property was to be distributed to the poor of the village by the trustees of Pridgeon's Charity.

By 1853 these five charities, plus Fen Allotments, were merged into one and became known as The Poor Charity. In 1880 the surviving trustees of this charity were Rev Joseph Holmes, vicar of Swineshead; Robert Shaw, farmer; John Cooper, grazier; Richard Harrison, farmer and grazier, all of Swineshead; and Richard Ingall, grazier, of Gibbet Hills. In a Charity Commission document dated 17th December 1880, seven new trustees were nominated; William Durston Bagg, farmer; John Harrison Brown, farmer; William Conway Hine, surgeon; Abraham Jackson, farmer; Charles Hambleton Sharpe, farmer and land agent; Robert Delanoy Cooke Shaw, farmer, and William Sparrow, farmer, all of Swineshead.

In 1701 Thomas Cowley of Donington by indenture, granted a messuage, or tenement, and barn with land, the rents of which were to provide £5 a year to pay a schoolmaster to teach ten poor children to read English; 20/- a year to buy books for the poor children; and 20/- a year to pay the curate of Swineshead for preaching a sermon every Tuesday in Easter Week forever. It was also to provide 2/- worth of bread every Sunday for a dozen poor inhabitants of Swineshead.

In 1720, Thomas Cowley, by his will of 20th August 1711, left land which besides providing funds for the upkeep of a school, also provided for distributing money, blankets, clothing and other necessities to the poor of Swineshead. In 1882 this charity was producing £186 a year, from which £90 was paid out for educational purposes, the rest being used to buy coal for the poor.

The Cowley Trust was formed to administer this benefactor's gifts via the Cowley Educational Foundation, and the Thomas Cowley Charity for the relief of the poor. On 2nd August 1858, an Act of Parliament confirmed the amended scheme of the Charity Commissioners for Cowley's Charity in the Parish of Swineshead. Richard Odlin Milson, surgeon, and Rev Joseph Watkins Barnes, clerk, both having left the district, were discharged as trustees, and the Rev Holmes and two farmers, John Cooper and Thomas Holmes, were made trustees.

Two bungalows in South Street, let at preferential rents, owe their existence to the William Gilding Memorial Fund. When William Gilding, a local farmer and parish councillor, died in February 1936, the whole village turned out to watch the cortege pass by. Five wagons full of flowers preceded the coffin. People stood in groups along the roads from Fenhouses, where Mr Gilding lived, all the way to the church. Cowley school children lined the road outside the school, and every house had its curtains drawn in respect. Many of those children, now in their eighties, still live in Swineshead and remember it well.

As he had been such a prominent and popular member of the village, it was proposed to erect a memorial to Mr Gilding. A village hall was suggested, and land near the Elephant & Castle Inn was given by Messrs Soames & Co the brewers, for this purpose. A meeting was held to approve the plans. The estimated cost of building the hall was £700 . There was to be ample parking space standing 50 feet back from South Street, and a design for the hall had been submitted to the Trustees of the William Gilding Memorial Fund. However, war was declared in 1939 and the hall was never built. The money was put to one side until after the war.

When the war ended it was decided that there was not enough money to build a village hall, so two bungalows were built in South Street, in conjunction with the Borough Council, and these are now let at a reduced rate to deserving tenants.

CHAPTER EIGHT

EDUCATION

Grammar schools had been in existence since medieval times, and by the Reformation were widespread throughout England. In the 16th century many public schools were founded, and like the grammar schools they concentrated on the teaching of latin grammar and religion. The mid sixteenth century saw the beginnings of education for the children of the poor in the 'song school' or 'reading school' for 'teching of pore mens children to rede and sing'. Later these schools developed to teach reading, writing and arithmetic. They were not widespread however and there is no record of any such establishment at Swineshead, though this does not preclude the possible existence of such a school in the area.

In 1699 The Society for Promoting Christian Knowledge was set up to promote the establishment of charity schools, and it also organised training colleges for teachers. In rural districts such as Lincolnshire the children were dependant on charity schools which local land owners endowed. These schools either admitted pupils freely or for a few pence per week.

In 1701 Thomas Cowley of Donington by indenture, granted a messuage, or tenement, and barn, with four parcels of land, the rents of which were to provide amongst other things, £5 a year to pay a schoolmaster to teach ten poor children to read English; and 20/- a year to buy books for the poor children. It is presumably about this time that Cowley's school began, with lessons in the church.

By his will of 1711, and codicil of 1718, Thomas Cowley left further land and property in Swineshead for the education of poor children, and for the relief of the poor in the parish. He died in 1720, leaving land which provided one hundred pounds a year for the upkeep of a school, and for an increase in the schoolmaster's salary to £10 per year. Cowley's School was, for more than a hundred years, housed in part of the Church. The west end of the south aisle was partitioned off from the rest of the church and initially accommodated around thirty girls and thirty boys. Their playground was the churchyard, or in wet weather the inside of the church.

Reportedly the first master of Cowley's school was Henry Lee. He was appointed on the 2nd March 1731 after signing the declaration:

> 'I, Henry Lee, being to be admitted to teach an English School within the Parish of Swineshead and elsewhere within the Archdeaconry of Lincoln do freely and voluntarily subscribe to the first and third articles and to the two former clauses of the second and also to the Declaration aforesaid this Second Day of March 1731. Stylo Anglio.' [Signed Henry Lee].

He also declared that he would conform to the Liturgy of the Church of England. Henry Lee continued as master until 1780, having served for forty nine years.

(One must query the view that Henry Lee was the first master. Presumably the school in the church was started shortly after 1701, and there must have been a teacher or teachers before Henry Lee. Furthermore, the codicil of 1718 in Thomas Cowley's will provided for an increase in the master's salary, so there must have been a master prior to that date).

Henry Lee's successor, Mr Turfitt, also served a long time, being master for forty-six years. Robert Turfitt was 'admitted and licensed to teach the Free School of Swineshead in the county and Diocese of Lincoln founded by Mr Cowley on 26th April 1780'. He was master until the school moved from the church to the new school building circa 1826. He was then eighty-three years old, and died in January 1827.

In 1825 the Trustees of Cowley's Charity bought a small plot of ground down Abbey Road to build a school. The National Society for Promoting the Education of the Poor in the Principles of the Established Church, (est 1811), gave a generous grant towards the cost of the building. The new school building accommodated 120 pupils of all ages. At that time most of the children left school round about the age of twelve, some even before reaching that age.

After Robert Turfitt retired he was probably replaced by George Stobie who is recorded as master in 1841. He was assisted by his wife, Barbara, and two mistresses, Mary Gill and Mary Hudson. He is recorded as schoolmaster on the 1851 census, and was then aged sixty-five. The census also records that he was born in Guernsey, and had, at that time, a school assistant, Frederick Jay, lodging with him.

The appointment of the masters and mistresses rested with the Trustees and, according to the rules in force in 1858, the schoolmaster had to be of good character, a member of the Church of England, and be able to teach the children reading, writing, English grammar and spelling, arithmetic, history, geography, land surveying and general science.

The prospective master or mistress was required to sign the following declaration:

'I. — declare that I will, when appointed, discharge always to the best of my ability the duties of master [or mistress] of the boys' [or girls'] school at Swineshead, and that in case I am removed or required to resign by the Trustees, I will acquiesce in such removal or requisition, and will thereupon relinquish all claim to the office and its future emoluments, and will deliver up possession of the school and residence to the Trustees.'

There were originally ten foundation scholars, five boys and five girls, who were selected from 'the poorest and most deserving children, resident in or belonging to the parish'. In addition to this the school was open to other poor children resident in the parish, between the ages of six and sixteen. These other children were required to pay a weekly sum 'not exceeding three pence per week . . . according to the respective circumstances and ages of the children'. These payments were made to the head teacher every Monday morning.

The master made an annual report in writing to the Trustees 'of the state of the school'. He also conducted an annual examination of the pupils, which took place in the presence of the Trustees, who distributed 'suitable prizes of small value' to the 'deserving children'. The school was also 'open to the visitation and inspection of Her Majesty's Inspector of Schools, and the Diocesan Inspector'.

By 1861 William Nixon and his wife were in charge of the school.

Attendance at school was often erratic depending upon the season, as children were often required to help with harvesting, and other land work, and this eventually led to regulatory legislation.

The Education Act of 1870 made it compulsory for every child to be provided with a place at an elementary school. To provide the necessary extra places board schools could be established to supplement the church schools.

The Agricultural Childrens Act in 1873, which was in part designed to overcome the lack of success of the 1870 Education Act, came into operation from 1st January 1875. This Act prohibited the employment of children under eight, and required children to attend school until at least the age of 12 or until they had passed a leaving examination.

The Education Act of 1876 made it compulsory for all children to attend school until the age of twelve. Poor attendance was still quite common. Then the Education Act of 1880 made school attendance compulsory until the age of fourteen, unless a pupil could pass the leaving examination.

In 1881 Cowley's school became a 'Senior Mixed Church of England School' and in January 1895, Mr Fryer Richardson, from Ramsey in Huntingdonshire, was appointed headmaster with four staff, including his wife Mary. The school then had 150 pupils. Mr Richardson soon acquired the reputation for being strict. He was the schoolmaster there for twenty-eight years, resigning as headmaster in 1923, as he had found it difficult to settle back into his job after his war service. (On his return from 'World War One' he was always known as Captain Fryer Richardson).

30. Swineshead Cowley School, Grade 3. 1923
On this photo are the following (but not in order).
Artie Burrell, Bill Stanwell, Stan Burrell, Len Mortimer, — — Gash,
Jack Bell, Stan Motson, Ernie Beck, Hugh Smithson, — — Bell,
Fred Woods, Tiny Beck, Joe Allgood, Len Gill, Tim Collishaw, — —
Blackburn, George Booth, Geoff Sharpe, and Colin Smith.

In 1896 the School Attendance Officer for the area was Robert Thorpe.

The Chairman of the School Managers in 1932 reported that the school was soon to become a 'Central School', under the Hadow Act. This recommended that children aged over eleven attending the older elementary schools should attend 'Central Schools'. Children from Swineshead, Swineshead Bridge, Fen Houses, and Wigtoft now attended the school. They were aged from seven to fifteen except those from Wigtoft who were all aged over eleven. Presumably Wigtoft was one of the 'older elementary schools'.

The headmaster in 1932 was Mr A E Corlett. The girls then learned cookery and housewifery as well as the three 'R's', and the boys learned handiwork, which included bookbinding. The school had a football team, a hockey team and a netball team. These sporting activities were financed by jumble sales and other fund raising events.

In 1952 Cowley's School became a Secondary Modern School, but in July 1965 it ceased to be such and became the Cowley's Foundation Aided Primary School, the older children then being sent to Cowley's Secondary School at Donington to finish their education. (It was the same benefactor, Thomas Cowley of Donington, who had provided for the establishment of schools at both Swineshead and Donington).

Other schools existed in Swineshead from the early part of the nineteenth century. 'Dame Schools' were privately run, often by a woman (frequently a widow or a spinster) who may not have been well educated herself, and parents paid for their children to attend these schools. There were quite a few of them in Swineshead. In 1849 Eleanor Gill ran a small day school in the village, and Mary and Elizabeth Hudson took boarders as well as day pupils. At North End James Dobney ran his day school, and there were two day schools at Gibbet Hills, respectively run by Mary Topham and Robert Johnson. In 1861 Mrs Mary Hopkins and Miss Alice Lumby were running a day school together.

A School Board was formed on 28th November 1879 leading to the building of a new infant school, and in 1881 this Board School for Infants was opened. Cowley's school then became a senior C of E school. The Board School was built to accommodate 120 children. Miss Martha Wright was the headmistress there until at least 1922.

Whites Directory for 1882 mentions a boarding and day school run by Mrs Mary Sophia Noble; and a private day school run by Thomas Johnson, who was also a land surveyor and agent to the Queen Fire & Life Insurance Co.

31. Swineshead Cowley Primary School. 1936

L. to R. back row: *Edwin Allett, Arthur Rickett, John Woods, Cyril Potter, − −Pacey, Jack Harwood.*

Middle row, standing: *Joan Haw, Freda Johnson, Ethel Linder, Joan Woods, Teresa Bell, − −Woods, Kathleen Freiston, Audrey Harrison, Betty Nevison. The teacher is Mr. Twells.*

Middle row, seated: *− −Woods, Joan Chadburn, Kathleen Harrison, Pearl Beck, Joyce Eaglan, Betty Wilson, Dorothy West.*

Front row, seated cross-legged: *Maurice Grantham, Patrick Oliver, Lewis Ulyatt, Norman Rainer, Bob Rawlinson, Ron Sharpe, Aubrey Penniston, Alfred May, Frank Freiston.*

121.

In 1932 Miss Johnstone was headmistress of the Infants School. There were only seventy-seven children attending by this time, forty-six staying for their lunch, which they brought with them. Miss Johnstone would also make them a milky Horlicks drink to go with their meal. The ages of the children then ranged from four to seven years.

In July 1958 when she retired, Miss Johnstone received a nest of walnut tables and an electric clock. Two other teachers, Mrs Stubley and Miss Harlock, both retiring at the same time, also received various gifts. As well as the leaving presents, each lady was presented with a bouquet by three of the children; Richard Gill, David Nundy and Julian Beecham.

The old infants' school, then a County Primary School, closed on 23rd July 1965 and the children were moved to the old Cowley School building in Abbey Road. They were later rehoused in a new school which was built next door. The old Cowley School building was then demolished.

CHAPTER NINE

CRIME

THE EARLIEST SUGGESTION OF CRIME in the village of Swineshead is the existence of a set of gallows in 1273. Presumably these stood in Gallows' Field, near Packhorse Lane, close to the place where the Stump Cross stands today. The gallows were owned by the Lord of the Manor, and in 1273 the Swineshead gallows were owned by Robert Grelley. Criminals could be hanged from these and left to swing in the wind as a deterrent to others.

Punishments varied throughout the ages and other forms of punishment used in medieval times were the stocks, the pillory which was similar to the stocks, and the whipping post. Confinement in Houses of Correction, or prisons, became a more usual form of punishment later on. These were also much used at the end of the sixteenth century for detaining vagrants. In the nineteenth century deportation was introduced.

32. An early drawing of Swineshead stocks in the Market Place. The Wheatsheaf Inn is in the background.

There is nothing to suggest that Swineshead was either particularly lawless or law abiding through the ages, and as in other towns and villages the threat of punishment was not a total deterrent to wrongdoing as the following cases illustrate:

In 1337 John de Podenhale stole twelve oxen from John de Holland at Swineshead. Again in 1339 John de Podenhale stole '14 large beasts from John de Hoyland of Swineshead'.

In 1338, John Crane of Swineshead murdered Godfrey son of Richard de Longholme of Swineshead. This murder took place in the village.

In September 1339, six quarters of beans worth 3s a quarter were sold to the abbot of Swineshead by William de Otteford, the keeper of the King's horses. He had obtained them as part of an unlawful fine he had imposed on the people of Donington.

The monks themselves were sometimes lured into temptation as the story of Ralf de Byker shows, when in 1401 he absconded from the abbey after having been found guilty of stealing, and of assaulting a former abbot. (For more detail of this incident, see chapter two).

The Court Rolls of The Manor of the Moor record the following cases tried and fined in the middle of the seventeenth century:

In 1636 George Riley was fined 3s 4d for 'sufferinge his sheepe to goe in Gallowe Field without a Tenter (contrary to custome).'

In 1639 Nicholas Mowbray was fined 2s 4d for 'steepinge or Wateringe hempe by the highe way, to the annoyance of passengers.'

In 1641 'John Storer the elder of Swineshead for Courseinge of hares within this Mannor without Licence and leave of the Lord.' was fined 6s 8d.

John Beaver was fined 18d in 1647 for 'brewinge and puttinge to sale unholsome Beere and therefore to forfeit to the Lord of this Mannor.'

In these early days law and order was represented by the Parish Constable. He was generally a small farmer or tradesman or householder who was required to take on the post, unpaid, for one year. This was not always a satisfactory system as sometimes the constable would turn a blind eye towards any offences committed by his friends and family. Furthermore it became increasingly common for the nominal holder of the post to pay others to do the job for him.

Common complaints against a person could be taken to the Holland Quarter Sessions. In 1683, William Yates of Swineshead appeared before the magistrates accused of failing to maintain Mary Okes, as he had promised to do during her lifetime, in return for the profits of her lands. After a year of maintaining her as promised, he had turned her over to the parish whilst retaining the profits from her lands.

Also in 1683 George Michell gent, of Swineshead, appeared before the court because of his refusal to accept John Risebrooke as his apprentice. It was decided that Michell should be discharged of the boy but should have 'another more sound and convenient for him' within the next three months. Another similar instance, in the same year, of refusal to accept an apprentice is the case of John Gouldice, yeoman. He did not wish to take a girl, Anna Massey, as a pauper apprentice, and for refusing to do so was fined ten shillings. (In both cases these were pauper apprentices, ie young people apprenticed at the parish charge. The apprenticeships lasted until the age of twenty four, giving the employer ten years of service merely for the cost of their keep. The parish officers could require employers to accept such apprentices. In reality such apprentices were often nothing more than domestic drudges).

In 1683 a charge was brought against Henry Gray, a labourer living in Swineshead, for the theft of two saucepans, one pewter and one brass, belonging to John Hickson. Gray confessed and was flogged for his crime.

Over the years the Quarter Sessions records contain a litany of similar offences too numerous to mention here, but to conclude here are two more of later date:

In 1832 Thomas Smith and John Lighton were charged with offering base coins at the Wheatsheaf public house at Swineshead statute on the 7th May. One man had eight half crowns and one sovereign of counterfeit coin in his possession when apprehended.

William Jefford of Swineshead, blacksmith, in 1833 was found guilty of assaulting Charles George Mastin and was sentenced to six months imprisonment in the House of Correction at Spalding. He was also fined £10 and was to be further imprisoned until it was paid.

Early nineteenth century Lincolnshire had a rapidly rising population. Many people were seeking work in the area as navvies for the drainage projects, on the building of the railway or as land workers at harvest time. The unpaid parish constable could no longer be expected to cope with the rising crime, and in 1836 salaried parish constables were introduced. This was the only form of policing for the next twenty years until in 1856 the Lincolnshire Constabulary was formed when an Act was passed making it compulsory for each county to have a police force.

Before this time other forms of crime prevention were tried. 'The Swineshead Association for the Prosecution of Felons and for the Mutual Protection of Property' was established in 1792. It met annually at The Griffin Inn. Anyone wishing to join and living within a twelve mile radius of Swineshead, paid a subscription of 5/-, plus 5/- more for up to sixty acres of land. Anyone possessing over sixty acres was charged three halfpence per extra acre. The formation of this Association reflected the lack of adequate policing, and the need for self-help. The benefits included: 'payment for a stolen horse—one half its value up to a certain amount; and for beast, sheep and swine, three quarters of the animal's value'.

At a meeting of this Association on 3rd December 1868, it was announced that in 'the last twenty-seven years there has been paid for 110 Sheep slaughtered, and one Beast poisoned, £166 8s'. The subscribers at this date numbered thirty-six and the funds amounted to £229 1s 2d. Among the subscribers were Rev Holmes, John Cooper, William Reddish, Zebadee Jessop and W Ingall.

In the first half of the 1800s it was possible to be deported for various offences. Several men from Swineshead were sent to the colonies: William Johnson of Swineshead, aged twenty-three, was

FOUR GUINEAS

REWARD !

Swineshead Association for the Prosecution of Felons, and the Mutual Protection of Property.

WHEREAS some evil disposed person or persons did, last Night, (Monday,) wilfully

BREAK SEVERAL PANES OF

GLASS

In the windows belonging to MR. JOHN JESSOP.

NOTICE IS HEREBY GIVEN, that a Reward of Four Guineas will be paid to the person or persons who will give such information as shall lead to the conviction of the offender or offenders ; Two Guineas to be paid by the said MR. JOHN JESSOP, and Two Guineas by

W. D. REDDISH,

Treasurer of the Association.

Joseph S. Barwick, Printer and Stationer, 48, High Street, Boston.

33. An undated reward poster, possibly c. 1870

sentenced to seven years at Holland Quarter Sessions on the 3rd July 1833. His crime had been to steal four silver spoons from William Broughton. Jane, William Broughton's wife, gave evidence along with Ann Clare, George Barton, and John Bucknell, all of Swineshead. The village constable, Edward Watson, also gave evidence against Johnson, who was found guilty. He was sent to New South Wales on board *Lloyds* in 1833. His partner in crime, Reuben Wartnaby, was also sentenced to be ' . . . Transported beyond the Seas for Seven Years'.

Thomas Elliott, aged eighteen, was sentenced at the Holland Quarter Sessions on 18th October 1847. The indictment read:

> 'Against Thomas Elliott late of Swineshead Labourer for having on the 17th day of August 1847 within the parts of Holland feloniously stolen one gelding of the price of ffive Pounds of the goods and chattels of George Houcher. The said Thomas Elliott being arraigned pleaded not guilty - Guilty on Trial - Sentenced to be transported beyond the Seas for Ten Years.'

He sailed in 1853 on the *Rodney* to Van Diemen's Land (Tasmania). The years between the trial and the actual departure for the colonies were usually spent on the hulks on the Thames at London.

Thomas Banks of Swineshead, aged twenty-eight, was found guilty of stealing twelve bushels of wheat worth 36s and five sacks of wheat worth 10s, from Tunnard Aspland of Swineshead on 26th March 1846. He also stole one sack of wheat worth 2s from Robert Shaw. Banks had a previous conviction for a felony in 1839, and was sent to Van Diemens's Land.

Another offence committed by two men, James Leeson and Reuben Martin, was the theft of 'twelve pounds weight of Leather of the value of two shillings and one pair of boots of the value of six shillings' from William Sparrow of Swineshead. The men, both labourers, were accused of breaking into the premises of William Sparrow on 27th January 1843. Leeson pleaded guilty but Martin pleaded not guilty. However Martin was found 'Guilty on Trial' and they were both transported for seven years. These two men were tried at different times, James Leeson on 3rd April 1843, and Reuben Martin on 2nd January 1844.

In 1839 Francis Ward of Swineshead, aged seventeen, was convicted at Holland Quarter Sessions and sentenced to seven years imprisonment for stealing clothing. He served his time on a Thames hulk at Deptford and was pardoned on 2nd February 1843 after serving only part of his sentence. He then stole one cwt. of hair at Bourne and was sentenced at Kesteven Quarter Sessions on the 1st July 1844. He was deported for ten years and sailed on *Hyderabad* in 1845 to Norfolk Island Penal Colony.

Other young men from Swineshead found guilty of a crime and sentenced to deportation were John Holland, aged twenty-nine, who received a life sentence in 1836, and was deported in 1837 to Van Diemen's Land; William Read, aged twenty-one in 1837, who was given a life sentence, and sailed for New South Wales in 1838; and John Davis alias Davison, who was sentenced to seven years at the age of twenty-five in 1837, and sailed to New South Wales the following year.

In 1766 the first meeting was held to propose the enclosure of the Eight Hundred Fen, and the following year there were petitions presented against the enclosure. There was other opposition however which took the form of rioting. At Holland Quarter Sessions of 29th July 1768, three Swineshead men appeared to answer a complaint by Henry Robinson, also of Swineshead. He accused Edward Burton, of Swineshead, butcher; Thomas Ingall of Swineshead, innkeeper; and John Handson Junior of Swineshead, farmer; together with James Campbell, Matthew Likely and Daniel Cook, also of Swineshead, 'and divers other persons (who) did commit a Riot and Tumult at Swineshead and break the window and attempt to pull down part of the Dwelling House there of the said Henry Robinson'. Also involved in this riot were Joseph Buswell, heckler; Robert Mutton, butcher; Richard Grainger, tailor, all of Swineshead. Recognizances were taken for their appearance at the next sessions and for their good behaviour until then.

At the October Sessions Edward Burton 'submitted to the said Indictment and his fine was set at £20, and he the said Edward

Burton not paying the said twenty pounds was ordered to be committed to the gaol. . . .' As for the others, Daniel Cook, James Campbell, Matthew Likely, Joseph Burwell, Robert Mutton and Richard Grainger, they were discharged not having had any further complaint made against them. Presumably Henry Robinson was an active supporter of the Enclosure Act and so incurred the wrath of its opponents.

In June 1768 a mob which had assembled at Hubbert's Bridge walked into Boston intent on rioting. There they broke into the office of Mr E Draper, Attorney at Law, to seize enclosure documents which they then destroyed. They also threatened to destroy the house of Robert Barlow, a merchant in the town, unless he promised to withdraw his support for enclosure. They similarly threatened Mr Tunnard and Mr Yerburgh both of Frampton. It is almost certain that the rioters were led by a person known as 'Gentleman Smith' of Swineshead.

At the July 1768 Sessions John Hiskins of Swineshead, labourer; William Rawsley late of Brothertoft, labourer; George Kelks of Swineshead, labourer; and John Smith of Swineshead, grazier were indicted 'for committing a Riot'. When they appeared as required at the next Sessions the first three mentioned were discharged. There is no mention of Smith who presumably failed to appear.

At the April Sessions William Smith gent, of Swineshead, had given cognizance for the appearance of John Smith, grazier, at the July 1768 Sessions, even though John failed to appear.

In this same month, July 1768, a meeting was held by a number of landowners at Sleaford who resolved to defeat the rioters when they next assembled, and to arrest their leaders. They engaged some drainage labourers to confront the rioters. The confrontation took place at Kirton Holme, but the drainage labourers took no action as they were greatly outnumbered, the number of rioters being put at about a thousand, though such a large number may have been an over estimation.

On 20th July 1768 Sir J Cust, Sir C Frederick, and Mr Yerburgh of Frampton, with about twenty armed men rode into Boston intent on confronting some insurgents. For 'it had been concerted by the insurgents, before Smith surrendered, to fire Boston.' The Scots Greys, at that time stationed in Boston for the purpose of preventing such disturbances, forced the armed band of men to withdraw, and prevented the rioters, led by Smith, from firing the town.

At the Quarter Sessions of May/June 1769 Edward Draper of Boston, gent, appeared 'to prosecute George Atkin of Swineshead, labourer, for a Riot and misdemeanour'. 'For the like offence as George Atkin' Edward Draper also prosecuted 'Elizabeth Bragden, maid to Samuel Lamb at Brothertoft; Edward Cheeseman, of Swineshead, tailor; John Waltham of Sibsey, labourer; the wife of Robert Allen, Kirton, grazier; Eden Simpson, servant maid to Robert Gray of Wyberton, grazier; William Dickinson of Swineshead, labourer; John Killion of Swineshead, labourer; John Oliver of Swineshead, labourer; John Wood of Quadring, labourer; and William Hopkinson of Swineshead, labourer.'

From this time until 1774 there were several such disturbances:

1770.
Mr J Tunnard had about 50 sheep hamstrung.
At Hart's Grounds a barn was burnt down.
At Brothertoft, John Hobson had a mare hamstrung.
Messrs Tunnard and Yerburgh had some hay burnt.
Herbert Ingram of Boston had a horse shot.
Robert Creasey of the old Ferry House had ewes and lambs killed.
On Pelham's Plot a house was burnt down.
Robert Barlow had two horses poisoned, as had Mr Garfitt, merchant.
In July most of the gates erected to enclose the fen were destroyed.
In November, John Woods of Swineshead was shot dead to prevent him turning informer.
Mr J Wilks, commander of Sir C Frederick's guard at Brothertoft was shot through a window shutter. He was badly wounded in the face and lost an eye.

1771.
At Brand End Stephen Carnal of Swineshead had a new barn and a harvested crop of oats destroyed by fire.

Mr Simpson of Heckington had a barn and about 50 lasts of oats
burnt, for enclosing a piece of land in Holland Fen.

Mr T Wright of Algarkirk had a barn and stable set on fire. Mr
Clayton of Fosdyke Inn had a stack of hay fired.

1772.

A shot was fired into the sitting room of Mr Watson at Kirton and a
letter left threatening to shoot him.

Gabriel Tunnard and Edward Monk, of Frampton, each had a stack
burnt.

At Clay Hills a barn and a house were attacked by four or five
armed men who shot a man through the foot as he lay in bed. One
of the attackers, John Tunnard, was killed by a shot from the
house.

1774.

Mr Blackwith of Frampton had a barn burnt down.

Mr Emmerson of Kirton had a hovel and a waggon burnt.

A shot was fired through the window of Robert Barlow's house in
Boston, hitting Mrs Barlow in the head.

Whilst great numbers of people were involved in these riots and
disturbances, it is generally held that William Smith, alias
'Gentleman' Smith, of Swineshead or Kirton Holme, was the
'captain of the leaders'. But surprisingly, in 1772, he turned
King's evidence, against an alleged former accomplice in the
murder of John Woods in 1770. The story is best told in the words
of Marrat who had the details from a Mr Johnson, school-master,
of Kirton:

> The beginning of July produced an extraordinary affair
> respecting the above transaction; W Smith, of Kirton Holme,
> either through fear of being impeached or in hopes of
> obtaining a great reward, went to London and there deposed,
> before Sir John Fielding, that he was in company with John
> Tunnard, and that he and one Crampton, were the three
> persons that beset the house of John Woods, of Swineshead,
> November 21st 1770, and that Tunnard was the man who
> shot the said Woods. Being (says Mr Johnson, late
> schoolmaster of Kirton, to whose manuscripts we are
> indebted for this account) on the inquest, I had an

opportunity of seeing how the poor fellow was mangled; part of his skull was blown into the chimney corner and stuck in the wall. August the 10th, 1772, the assizes at Lincoln began, when W Smith appeared as King's evidence against Crampton, who was arraigned, on the Coroner's inquest for the murder of John Woods, of Swineshead. The Counsel for the Crown set forth in their pleadings, that Crampton was concerned with another person in the said murder, who was admitted King's evidence. W Smith the accomplice, proved it is said, that himself and Crampton went to Woods' house about eight o'clock at night, and at the distance of about four yards, discharged a gun, loaded with large shot, which blew his skull to pieces, and that he died immediately. The fact against the prisoner was fully proved, but we must observe that the whole weight of the evidence rested entirely on the oath of the accomplice. Crampton was called upon for his defence, when to the surprise of all present, he set up an alibi, supported by the oaths of two witnesses, who deposed that in the evening the murder was committed, that he (Crampton) was many miles distant from the place where the murder was perpetrated from the hour of five till eleven at night. The judge summed up the proceedings, and lamented that no evidence could be found to strengthen that of the accomplice, on which account he left the prisoner in the power of the jury, who after half an hours consultation, brought him in Not Guilty.'

Footnote: As regards administrators of the law, Swineshead had a Justice of the Peace living at Swineshead Hall in High Street. His name was James Edwin-Cole Esq FRHS, JP, Barrister at Law, who styled himself the 'Duke of Polignano'. It is not clear how he acquired this title, but an entry in 'Whitaker's Peerage', of 1915, lists him as sixth Duke, son of the fourth Duke and brother of the fifth. He was born in 1835 in Wigtoft and his title of Duke of Polignano was established in 1905. Polignano is a small town on the east coast of Italy a few miles south of Bari. James Cole lived at Swineshead Hall from at least 1882 until the early part of the twentieth century.

CHAPTER TEN

SOCIAL LIFE AND RECREATION

B EFORE THE TWENTIETH CENTURY the annual holiday, if any, and the few public holidays and Sundays, were the extent of social and recreational life outside the normal working week. Evenings, after the working day, were another opportunity for leisure, but tiredness after a hard day's work, and lack of money restricted any leisure activities. Holidays and feast days were looked forward to with anticipation. Market day, with its bustle and crowds, provided some with opportunities for meeting other people and exchanging news. Even the annual hiring day, when farm labourers and domestic servants made themselves available for hire, was a social event and looked forward to with some eagerness.

Swineshead had had a market every Thursday since the early twelfth century, and market day would give many people an opportunity to meet their neighbours and to exchange news and gossip.

A Fair was held in Swineshead from 1292, when the abbot of Swineshead was granted a licence to hold a fair there on October 2nd each year. This fair was for the sale of cheese and onions, and was held on what is now known as Cheese Hill. It was still being held in 1896. Another fair, held on the first Thursday in June, was for the sale of cattle.

These fairs would be exciting events for the locals, for not only was there the usual commerce but there would be entertainments of all kinds. Sometimes groups of travelling players would set up their stall somewhere and act out plays. In the sixteenth century, Swineshead had its own group of travelling players, whose costumes were provided by the parish. They took their plays around the neighbouring villages and they are recorded as having played in Sutterton in the early part of the 1500's, when they afterwards took a collection and raised nine shillings and six pence. In 1636, because of an outbreak of the plague, all fairs were cancelled.

In the early part of the twentieth century, a puppet show called Tiller's Mannequins, would occasionally provide entertainment in the market place. This show was run by a local travelling family, who came to Swineshead regularly before the 1914-18 war. They would sometimes hold a singing competition and on occasions would offer a prize such as a pig. After an absence during the war the show returned for a while before finally disappearing. Another event taking place about the same time was Barwick's Spring Fair with stalls and roundabouts.

One informant recalls another annual entertainment known locally as 'Swineshead Statis' which was held in the paddock of the Green Dragon, and included entertainments such as stalls and a coconut shy. This would be the Swineshead statute held in May each year. As the word 'statute' can mean hiring fair it is probable that 'Swineshead Statis' was a relic of such an event, continuing after the practice of public hiring had died out.

On 3rd July 1897 Swineshead Annual Show was held in Mr Evans field behind the Green Dragon inn. The Brass Band played and there was dancing in the evening. The show was held yearly until 1932, when due to waning support and financial losses, it was decided to end this event which had once been so popular. It had previously been one of the largest agricultural shows in the county.

The only other time Swineshead experienced a show of this type was when it acted as host to the Lincolnshire Show. On 16th and 17th of June 1954, the Lincolnshire Show was held in the Abbey grounds. In those days the Lincolnshire Show did not have its own permanent show ground, and was sited at a different venue each year.

A more permanent facility was the Reading Room established at North End in 1895. There was also a reading room and small library in South Street which was demolished to make way for a modern bungalow in the 1960's. Reading Rooms offered periodicals and newspapers to read, as well as somewhere to meet friends. One of these was originally a social club, the funds for which were raised by the villagers with the encouragement of Mr Fryer Richardson, the schoolmaster. This social club later became the Cottage Reading Room.

Another opportunity for socialising was provided by the Friendly Societies, although their principal aim was to provide a form of social security. There were a number of Friendly Societies in Swineshead. In 1913 these included the Independant Lodge of Foresters (Flower of Swineshead Lodge, No 842, secretary Maurice Johnson), with 226 members and a fund of £1,600; The Oddfellows (Kingston Unity Lodge, secretary Fryer Richardson), which had 156 members and a fund of approximately £300; and an Independant Benefit Society (secretary W Morris) with 126 members and a fund of £600. In addition there were various sick and dividing societies connected with some of the public houses in the village.

Friendly Societies date back to 1687, when a Friendly Society was founded at Bethnal Green. They were the original form of social security, providing sick pay and funeral expenses when needed. It was laid out in the Articles of the Society how much each member should pay, and what a person should receive, if and when sick. On his death a widow would receive money towards her husband's funeral expenses.

As an attraction to ensure the attendance of all members, the monthly meetings were often held at one of the local inns. Each member was required to pay a weekly sum at the meeting, part of which was paid to the landlord for 'refreshments'. Members who failed to attend the meeting were still required to pay their dues, and those who were present drank the absentees share of the ale. Naturally most men were loathe to pay and not attend, so attendances were usually high!

Some Societies also held an Annual Feast which was usually held on the club's anniversary. These feasts were exciting events eagerly anticipated. The members would meet at their usual meeting place, wearing their regalia, and march in procession to

SWINESHEAD
Foresters' Jubilee Anniversary,
THURSDAY, MAY 15TH, 1890.

ATHLETIC SPORTS.

EVENTS:

No. 1.- QUARTER-MILE OBSTACLE RACE (Open).
Twice round the course. FIRST PRIZE, £1 1s.,
SECOND, 7s., THIRD, 3s. Entrance Fee 9d.

No. 2.—100 YARDS BUCKET-AND-WATER RACE
(Open).—Competitors to carry on their heads an
ordinary Bucket three-parts filled with water, which
must contain *not less* than One-gallon on reaching the
winning-post. FIRST PRIZE 6s. SECOND 4s. THIRD 2s.
Entrance Fee 6d.

No. 3 —QUARTER-MILE FLAT RACE (for Members
of Forester's Society only.—Twice round the course.
FIRST PRIZE, 12s., SECOND, 5s., THIRD, 2s. 6d.
Entrance 6d.

No. 4 —WALKING THE GREASY POLE (Open).—
Competitors to walk barefoot across a pole laid one
foot above water without help from their hands.
PRIZE, Half-a-Guinea (in money). Entrance 6d.

No. 5.—ONE MILE FLAT RACE (Open).—Eight
time- round the course. FIRST PRIZE, £1 1s.,
SECOND, 10s., THIRD, 5s. Entrance 9d.

No. 6.—120 YARDS JUVENILE RACE (OPEN).—
For youths under 14.—FIRST PRIZE, 6s., SECOND,
4s., THIRD, 2s. Entrance 6d.

No. 7.—100 YARDS EGG RACE (Open).—Competitors
to carry the Egg in a spoon carried in their mouths,
with hands tied behind. FIRST PRIZE, 5s., SECOND
2s. 6d. Entrance 6d.

No. 8.—QUARTER-MILE (OPEN) FLAT RACE.—
Twice round the course. Value FIRST PRIZE, 15s.,
SECOND, 6s. THIRD, 3s, Entrance 6d.

No. 9.—100 YARDS (OPEN) MARRIED WOMENS'
RACE.—Competitors to peel two potatoes at 50 yards
from winning post. FIRST PRIZE 7s., SECOND, 3s.
Entrance 6d.

No. 10.—HALF-MILE FLAT RACE.—(For agricultural
Labourers—Competitors to be over 30 years of age.)
FIRST PRIZE, 12s., SECOND, 5s., THIRD, 2s. 6d.
Entrance 6d.

No. 11.—100 YARDS (OPEN) SINGLE WOMENS'
RACE.—Competitors also to wind up 50 yards of
worsted. FIRST PRIZE, 5s., SECOND 2s. 6d.
Entrance 6d.

No. 12.—120 YARDS (OPEN) FLAT RACE.—FIRST
PRIZE, 15s. SECOND, 6s. Entrance 6d.

Articles will be given to the full value of the Prizes
mentioned.

SPECIAL.—If less than Three entries be made for any
event no race will be run ; If less than Five no
Third Prize will be given, and if less than Four
no Second Prize will be offered.

M. J. JOHNSON, *Hon. Sec.*

JOHNSON, PRINTER, SWINESHEAD,

*34. A Jubilee sports programme
of 1890.*

the church following a brass band. After the service they would then parade around the village carrying a banner. Lunch would be held at the inn, and would usually take the form of a roast beef dinner with, of course, some ale. Occasionally these feasts would include music and dancing.

All members were expected to attend the other members' funerals and some clubs would fine men for not doing so. This was not often necessary as funerals were also looked upon as feasts, since they were generally followed by a supper.

The Swineshead Oddfellows Society owned six acres of land down Church Lane which had been turned into allotments for their members. This land was sold around 1986 as modern day members no longer required land for allotments. The Swineshead Parish Council also owned allotments in the village and was reputed to be one of the first councils to take advantage of the Allotment Act of 1908. They had purchased eighteen acres and turned them into sixteen allotments. Each allotment was approximately 1 acre. (An allotment was 'part of a field divided between a number of tenants mainly to cultivate for food for themselves and their families', and was quite different to the 'allotments' made during the Enclosures). Some of these council allotments were in Fenhouses, but they have now been sold. The council still has eighteen acres down Villa Lane near Asplands Barn, which are divided into half acre and one acre lots.

Swineshead's Friendly Societies were very active and reports appeared regularly in the newspapers of their various activities. On May 15th 1890, to celebrate their society's Jubilee, the Swineshead Foresters held a Sports Day. The various events included a quarter-mile obstacle race (first prize £1.1s), walking the greasy pole, and 100 yards bucket-and-water race. The latter required the competitors to carry on their heads a bucket which was three-quarters full of water, of which they must have at least one gallon left on reaching the winning post. First prize for this was 8s. There was also a married women's race, requiring the entrants to peel two potatoes at least 50 yards from the winning post; and a single women's race which required the ladies to wind up 50 yards of worsted.

Seven years later the village celebrated Queen Victoria's Diamond Jubilee, when it was reported in the Boston Guardian dated 26th June 1897, that on the previous Sunday morning the church bells rang out and the Swineshead Brass Band played 'God Save the Queen' at the end of the service (see photograph overleaf). The following Tuesday was declared a holiday in the village and many people decorated their houses. At one o'clock the church bells rang out and at two o'clock there was a gathering in the Market Place, where the school children sang 'God Save the Queen', after which a procession of farm wagons filled with the children and headed by the Brass Band progressed through the village. The procession stopped at various places and sang hymns. Afterwards a 'substantial meat tea' was provided by Mr Waldegrave of the Griffin Inn, in a marquee which had been erected in Mr John Sparrow's field. About 1200 people were catered for and food was sent to the homes of the old people who were too infirm to attend. In the evening there were games and dancing to the Swineshead Band.

35. Swineshead Brass Band leaving a fête held in Tyler's field near Tarry Hill. Possibly the Diamond Jubilee celebrations of 1897.

In the nineteenth century people worked long hours and would be tired at the end of the day. After his evening meal a man might tend his small garden, by way of recreation, albeit a necessary one, or go down to the inn for a beer. Swineshead had numerous inns and beerhouses over the years, some of which are still in existence.

The Wheatsheaf in the Market Place, which is late Georgian, was a drovers inn, as was the Leagate (Leeds Gate) at Coningsby, and the Ferryboat Inn at Langrick. In 1849, when John Jessop was the landlord of the Wheatsheaf, it also had its own brewery. In 1896 The Wheatsheaf was run by Joseph Whitworth, who was also a potato merchant and kept the posting house where letters were received and sent out. In 1913 Ernest Callow Stammers, who was also a butcher, and the agent for Nottingham Brewery Ltd, was the landlord. Most innkeepers had other jobs as the inn did not usually bring in sufficient to keep a wife and family.

In the nineteenth century the Wheatsheaf had its own brewery which, according to one informant, was situated in Church Lane on the site of the house now known as Westholme. This lane was once called Brewery Lane. The 1891 census shows the brewer, Robert Smith, living there with his wife, Martha, and a large family of seven sons and five daughters, all between the ages of three and twenty four. The Griffin Inn also had its own brewery and as it was situated at the corner of Brewery Lane and Church Street (now known as High Street), it is possible that the brewery at Westholme could have been associated with The Griffin.

The following advert was printed in the Stamford Mercury in 1887:

```
┌─────────────────────────────────────────────────────┐
│               WHEAT SHEAF BREWERY                    │
│          SWINESHEAD - ESTABLISHED 1830               │
│                                                      │
│     The Celebrated Swineshead ALES and STOUT, in     │
│                       casks                          │
│          of 6,9,18,26, and 54 Gallons each.          │
│       X    ALE              0. 10    per Gall        │
│       XX   "                1.  0     "    "         │
│       XXX  "                1.  2     "    "         │
│       STOUT                 1.  2     "    "         │
│                                                      │
│                Post card will find                   │
│     J. BRAMLEY, Wheat Sheaf Brewery, SWINESHEAD      │
└─────────────────────────────────────────────────────┘
```

The Green Dragon in the Market Place, was kept by John Elliott in 1849, but by 1896 was being run by Albert Sparrow. In 1913 The Green Dragon had a landlady, Mrs Isabella Evans, and again in 1922 when Mrs Lucy Morriss ran it. By 1933 William Frederick Trevor was the landlord.

The Black Bull in the Market Place was kept by Penelope Nunnery in 1849. From 1881 to 1896 Samuel Middlebrooke was the landlord, and may still have been there when a traveller passing through Swineshead at the turn of the century recommended The Bull as being 'a capital centre for tourists and cyclists with every accommodation.'

The Black Swan stood on High Street near Tarry Hill, but there had been a former public house called The Swan, said to be on Tarry Hill. In 1849 George Monks was the landlord of The Swan (Tarry Hill) but two years later it was being run by his wife Mary. In 1881 Richard Brown and his wife Jemima, were the licensees. In 1891 Tom Mason was the landlord and his widowed mother Rebecca, who lived there with him, helped him to run it as Tom was also a farmer. In 1913 John Middlebrooke was landlord and in 1933 Mrs Charlotte Middlebrooke was the landlady. (Just when it closed and the Black Swan took over is not clear).

In 1888 the Boston Guardian newspaper, dated 21st January, reported that the landlord of The Red Lion Inn at Swineshead, John William Rawlinson, had been summoned for permitting drunkeness on his premises. On January 6th Police Constable Kempstone had visited The Red Lion where he found a man named Richard Beck lying on the floor in front of the fire. Beck got up and left the inn, staggering down the street. Despite the landlord's denials of supplying the man with alcohol, and the evidence of another customer who said the man was just sleeping by the fire, Beck was fined £4 plus £1.4s.6d costs, and Rawlinson had his licence endorsed.

South Street had two inns; The Royal Oak and The Elephant & Castle. The latter was a comparatively new establishment, first being mentioned in White's Directory in 1896. In 1913 it belonged to Soames Brewery and the licensee was Robert Francis Horn. The Royal Oak seems to have been a beer house only.

The Golden Cross at North End was kept by George Rawlinson in 1881. It stayed in this family for a number of years, Mrs Rachel Rawlinson being the landlady in 1913. By 1933 George Alfred Pordham was the landlord.

There was also at one time a public house called the New Inn at North End, which stood on the opposite side of the road to the Golden Cross but a few yards further along. It closed just after the

Second World War, some time in the 1940's.

In 1849 The Barge at Swineshead Bridge, or Fortyfoot Bridge as it was then known, was run by William Drury. In 1913 The Barge, then known as The Railway Hotel, was run by Richard Anthony Greetham. In 1933 it was still known as The Railway Hotel but was at that time run by Harry Morton Oliver. Just when it reverted to being called The Barge is uncertain.

The Plough on the Sleaford Road near Swineshead Bridge was run by Cornelius Dalton and his wife Emma between 1876 and 1881.

The Griffin, which was possibly the oldest public house in Swineshead, was demolished in the 1950's. It could have been named after the Griffin's head which formed part of the family crest of Sir John Lockton of the abbey. In 1849 the inn was kept by Henry Smith, who was also a brewer, and farmer of 34 acres, employing one labourer.

An interesting episode at the Griffin was reported in a Boston newspaper dated 5th October 1877:

INQUEST

Deputy Coroner Mr W J Pilcher, held an inquest on Friday on the body of Robert Henry Smith, landlord of the Griffin Inn, Swineshead. Mary Elizabeth Smith, daughter of the deceased said that on the 17th she noticed her father looking white on the lips as if some powder was on them. He seemed very ill and was taken into the parlour. She gave him some mustard and water and sent for the doctor. Mr M Pittard, a medical practitioner of Swineshead, said that he found the deceased quite unconcious and incapable of being roused. He had no doubt that he died from the effects of opium. Albert Sparrow, landlord of the Green Dragon Inn Swineshead, said Mr Smith went to see him about the purchase of some cabbage on the Wednesday and he then seemed very low and changed. George Morton, a travelling musician staying at the Griffin Inn said he was with the deceased at his death at 7.15 pm.

Verdict death by overdose of opium.'

Opium was widely used as a cure for the ague which caused shiverings and pain in the limbs, followed by thirst and fever. This illness, originally endemic in the fens, and believed to have been caused by the humid atmosphere, may have been a form of malaria. The standard cure, opium, was easily purchased over the counter in the local druggist's shop and over the years it became a habit as much as a cure, sometimes proving fatal, as in this case.

After Henry Smith's death The Griffin was run for a time by George Tomlinson from Redmile in Leicestershire. In 1896 Daniel Burton Waldegrave was the landlord, who the following year provided the feast for the Jubilee celebrations. In 1938, when Patrick Cassidy was the landlord, the Swineshead Bellringers used to dine there regularly each year, courtesy of Mr William Lawson Smith who was the Captain of the Bellringers.

One of the bellringers was Thomas Hinkins, who in 1936 was the sexton as well as being a bellringer (see *also Fig 11.* page 50). He was responsible for ringing a bell five minutes before each Sunday service. He succeeded Henry Dawson who had succeeded his father Samuel Dawson as sexton. Other bellringers at this time were Jack Bates, Len Gill, Ted Wilson, Thomas Wilson, Mr W L Smith, Charles Stubley and Arthur Randall.

In 1965 Mr Vernon Johnson, a local resident, left £100 for maintenance and renovation of the church clock. At this time Philip Reynolds had to wind the clock each night and to do so had to climb 56 stairs and 18 rungs of a ladder. Mr Johnson's bequest provided the clock with an automatic winder and Philip Reynolds was saved a nightly visit to the church.

Fig. 37 opposite. Swineshead members of 5th Boston Scouts.
L. to R. back row: *Albert Dawson, Dick Pordham, Ted Mowbray, Miss Young, Percy Middlebrooke, Len Pordham, Adolphus Brown, Evan Mason.*
Four in centre: *Bill Smith, Jack Smithson, Gib Hammond, Albert Smalley.*
Front row: *Rob Wright, — —, Stan Fox, J. Smalley, Cliff Taylor, — —.*

36. The Swineshead Avenue Football Team – 1910-11 season

37. Swineshead members of the 5th Boston Scouts. This photograph was taken at Swineshead Abbey about 1914. The scout mistress was Miss Hope Young of the Abbey. (See previous page for names.)

In 1907 the bellringers established a record by ringing the bells, with a full team, twice a day on each of the fifty two Sundays of the year. They almost repeated this feat the following year, but were prevented from doing so when heavy snow one evening made it impossible for some of the ringers to reach the church. The bellringers were Messrs Jack Bates, Mick Reynolds, Jack Cone, Thomas Wright, Luke Crampton, Harry Creasey, Willows Morriss, and James Edgoose. Mr Jack Bates was a bellringer for over 40 years.

At the end of the 1914-18 war many suspended social activities resumed again, and in 1919 on Wednesday 10th July, the Sunday School Festival was held once more. It was a warm sunny day and 'a very happy . . . band of scholars' gathered at the church at 2.00 pm, where 'the bells were ringing merrily'. The children

38. The first Sunday School outing after the end of the 1914-18 war. The children were paraded around the village on farm carts stopping for this photograph outside Len Grundy's butcher's shop.

climbed onto carts lent by various local farmers, and led by Swineshead Brass Band they walked in procession around the village, afterwards enjoying tea and sports. In the evening a dance was held on the vicarage lawn, for which there was an entrance fee of 1/-. The vicar at this time was Rev Hayes.

The Swineshead Brass Band was formed in 1886, when a meeting was held on 28th July at The Red Lion Inn. This meeting was attended by Messrs W Morgan, J L Nunnington, A R Sparrow, W S Barratt, F Cone, J Cone, W Cone, N Ceasar, J Favell, J Lind, J Woodward and F Greetham. Initially it was called Swineshead Brass Band, but by 1940 it had become known as Swineshead Silver Band.

The biggest problem for the newly formed band was the raising of money to buy instruments. It was proposed that 1/- should be paid on the first Saturday of September 1886, and 6d be paid on the first Saturday of each subsequent month. Anyone wishing to purchase their instrument outright had to pay an extra 6d.

The band was trained by Mr W Morgan of the gasworks, who said he would take the band on its first outing within six weeks. They must have all worked very hard as six weeks later the band marched in a torchlight procession from the gasworks to the market place, where they played the only four tunes they knew, one of which was 'God Save the King'. On this occasion the band consisted of the following: Mr Greetham, the Bandmaster, who played the first tenor horn; the secretary, Mr Middlebrook who played the cornet; Mr Hammond, Mr F Cone, Mr Harwood, Mr Richer and Mr Booth who all played cornets; Mr Favel, who played the bass drum; Mr Reast, who played second tenor horn; Mr Cone who played trombone; Mr Sparrow and Mr Thorpe who both played bass; and Mr J W Woods who played the side drum. That same year the band played Christmas carols in the market place.

Over the years the band meetings were held at various public houses in the village including The Red Lion, The Green Dragon, The Elephant & Castle and The Bull.

The band practised in a room at the rear of the Methodist Chapel, but during the second world war they had to move to a

GROUPS FROM COMMUNAL ACTIVITIES BETWEEN THE WARS

39. Swineshead members of the Boston Cub Pack (names opposite)

40. Swineshead Football Team. Season 1930-31 (Names opposite)

*41.	Children playing near the War Memorial in the Market Place probably shortly after its erection in 1920.	The Green Dragon is behind the memorial and the old Manor House is on the right.*

*42. The War Memorial as it is in the Market Place today, 1996, surrounded by mature shrubs and with railings around the area.	A seat is provided and the memorial sadly now carries names from the Second World War.*

39. L. to R., back row: Jack Clarke, Hubert Stanwell, Cyril Dawson, Rob Wright, Maurice Smalley, Sydney Scotney, Geoffrey Townsend.
Front row: Ray Townsend, Ray Horn, H. Hanson, Herman Lake, Gilbert Holmes, Arthur Pordham. Miss Hope Young was the leader.

40. L. to R., back row: Jack West, Albert Pordham, Ernest Smith, Bill Mowbray, George Pordham, Walter Tyler, George Curtiss, Harry Seymour.
Middle row: Albert Routen, Rob Wright, Ted Gilding, Arthur Burrell, Len Gill, Frank Gilding, − −Pordham, Frederick Trevor.
Front − seated on the floor: Raymond Horn and Arthur Ceasar.

barn in the Bandmaster's garden and then to the Wheatsheaf, where they rented a room. After the war they returned to the chapel room for a while until the chapel needed the room for its own use, and in 1960 money was raised to purchase the building now referred to as the band room in South Street.

Always popular, the band was kept busy playing for Garden Fetes, Parades, Galas, Dances, Christmas Carols, and events such as the Coronation or Jubilee celebrations. It was so popular at one time that it was necessary to split the band into two groups in order to fulfill all engagements. One of the band's regular commitments after the war was on Armistice Day when the bandsmen would march from The Golden Cross to the War Memorial in the Market Place at the head of a parade, where they played hymns and The Last Post, and then marched back to The Golden Cross. They then returned to the band room to prepare for a performance that same evening at the Chapel.

43. Swineshead Bowling Club c. 1934. (See opposite for names)

In May 1935, when Swineshead held its celebrations for the Silver Jubilee of George V, the band led an elaborate parade to start off the proceedings. Assembled in Church Avenue were the Parish Council, the British Legion, the Salvation Army, and a large group of schoolchildren. Preceded by the band they all marched to the church where a service was conducted by Rev C J Gurnhill and Rev W L Brooks of Kirton. After the service the procession marched to Tarry Hill where an oak tree was planted to commemorate the Jubilee. Councillor William Gilding planted the tree. The silver plated and engraved spade used by Mr Gilding was then presented to him by Councillor W L Smith, who thanked him for all his work during the last twenty one years as chairman of the Parish Council.

The procession returned to the Market Place and then to Cowley School, where tea was served to the children. Each child was presented with a Jubilee mug, and after tea childrens' sports were held in Mr Dawson's field behind the church. A whist drive and dance was held in the evening at Cowley School, the proceeds from which went to the Swineshead Nursing Association.

Another event of this kind was held in 1937 when a Coronation Bazaar was held on Saturday May 8th in the Salvation Hall, known locally as 'The Tin Tab', which stood next to the New Inn at North End. This was followed by a Musical Evening, admission by ticket only at a cost of 3d. Admission to the Bazaar had also cost 3d.

---

43. (opposite) This photograph was taken at the old bowling green behind The Green Dragon. In 1965 the club moved to the present premises in South Street.

L. to R. back row: R. Woods, — —Metcalf, Jesse Scotney, Len Grundy, Jack Smithson, Fred Trevor, Colin Smith, A. Routen, A. Bullock, Walt Tyler, Sid Houlder.

Second row: A. Corlett— —Dalton, — —Johnson, Fryer Richardson, William Gilding, — — — —, W. L. Smith, Geoff Dawson, Edward Mowbray, — — Horton.

Front row, seated: — — — —, R. Salter, — — — —, — — — —, — —Coppen, — — — —, F. Greetham.

The small boy in the front is unidentified.

In 1920 on November 13th, the Sunday nearest to Armistice Day, the unveiling and dedication ceremony of the Swineshead War Memorial took place. A dedication service was held before the unveiling and the church was 'packed to capacity'. The vicar Rev Hayes conducted the service assisted by Rev Jones, the Wesleyan Circuit minister. Hymns were sung and the Brass Band played. A procession marched from the church to the memorial led by the band and the choir, followed by relatives and comrades of the fallen, the school children and the general public.

William Gilding in his speech said that the memorial had cost £600 and some difficulties and mishaps had been encountered during its transportation on the railway. It had unfortunately been broken and some parts had had to be replaced, not all of

44. Swineshead Bowling Club members photographed at Boston Bowling Club, then behind the Peacock and Royal Hotel. c. 1952.
L. to R., back row: Geoff Dawson, Walter Mason, Bill Wadsley, George Burrell, Percy Tyler, Arthur Thorpe, Ted Mowbray.
Front row: Harry Eldred, Wilbert Bell, Colin Smith, Rob Wright, Cecil Beck.

which had arrived even then. He went on to say that it was intended to fence it in and plant shrubs and flowers around it, but the fence had not arrived yet either.

Lieutenant Colonel L H P Hart, D.S.O. and Bar, M.C., commanding the 4th Battalion Lincolnshire Regiment (TF) unveiled the memorial, and then addressed the crowd and distributed medals to the members of the forces who had returned.

William Gilding was the chairman of the Parish Council for many years, and was well known in Swineshead. He promoted a dance held annually on New Year's Eve at Cowley's School, which became known as 'Gilding's Dance'. Just about everyone in the village went to this dance, as it was considered to be a splendid affair. In 1932 Harry Payne's Orchestra, a well known dance band of the time, played to 200 people.

45. A typical wartime 'event' when 'Holidays at Home' were the rule rather than the exception. It also demonstrates the community spirit of a village— perhaps particularly evident in wartime. Since the majority of villagers knew, or at least knew of, everyone else, when a man or woman was in the forces they were a part of the village away from home. This was more evident than in towns where even men from the next street might be quite unknown to one another.

The Swineshead Silver Band played its part in helping to keep up spirits throughout the war.

153.

46. Swineshead Bellringers 1953.

L. to R. back row: Philip Reynolds, F. Porter, M. Randall, T. Wilson, J. Thorold. Front row: George Penniston, Jack Morriss (conductor) F. Bullock, D. Sharp.

There is no record of mummers, miracle plays, bare knuckle fights, cock fighting, and other ancient forms of entertainment in Swineshead, although some of these activities must surely have taken place there. And the children must have played at marbles, skipping, bowling the hoop, hop-scotch, and a host of other games such as Ring o' Roses, Oranges and Lemons, Farmer's Wife, and Piggy in the Middle, as children have done for generations. May they long continue to enjoy such simple games, and in so doing preserve some small part of their village's social history.

APPENDICES

APPENDIX 1

LOCKTONS OF THE ABBEY– FAMILY TREE.

This and the two succeeding tables.

(All dated baptisms, marriages, and burials were at Swineshead unless stated otherwise).

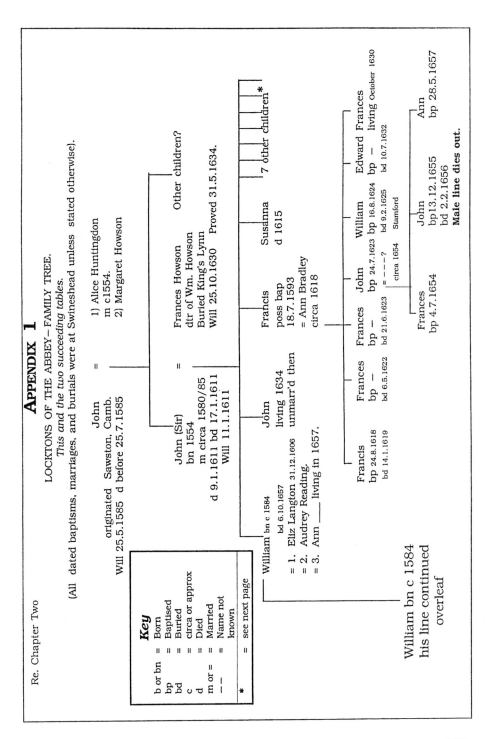

Key

b or bn = Born
bp = Baptised
bd = Buried
c = circa or approx
d = Died
m or = = Married
– – = Name not known
* = see next page

John
originated Sawston, Camb.
Will 25.5.1585   d before 25.7.1585

= 1) Alice Huntingdon
m c1554.
2) Margaret Howson

John (Sir)
bn 1554
m circa 1580/85
d 9.1.1611 bd 17.1.1611
Will 11.1.1611

= Frances Howson
dtr of Wm. Howson
Buried King's Lynn
Will 25.10.1630   Proved 31.5.1634.

Other children?

Francis
poss bap 18.7.1593
= Ann Bradley
circa 1618

John
living 1634
unmarr'd then

Susanna
d 1615

7 other children *

William bn c 1584
bd 6.10.1657
= 1. Eliz Langton 31.12.1606
= 2. Audrey Reading
= 3. Ann ____ living in 1657.

Francis
bp 24.8.1618
bd 14.1.1619

Frances
bp –
bd 6.5.1622

Frances
bp –
bd 21.6.1623

John
bp 24.7.1623
= – – –?
circa 1654

Frances
bp 4.7.1654

William bp 16.8.1624
bd 9.2.1625
Stamford

Edward
bp –
bd 10.7.1632

Frances
living October 1630

John
bp 13.12.1655
bd 2.2.1656
Male line dies out.

Ann
bp 28.5.1657

William bn c 1584
his line continued
overleaf

157.

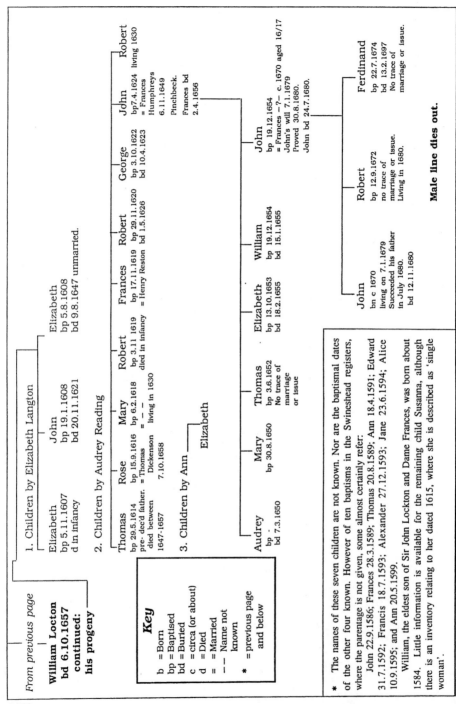

From previous page

William Locton
bd 6.10.1657
continued:
his progeny

1. Children by Elizabeth Langton

Elizabeth	John	Elizabeth
bp 5.11.1607	bp 19.1.1608	bp 5.8.1608
d in infancy	bd 20.11.1621	bd 9.8.1647 unmarried.

2. Children by Audrey Reading

Thomas
bp 29.5.1614
pre- decd father.
died between
1647-1657

Rose
bp 15.9.1616
= Thomas
Dickenson
7.10.1658

Mary
bp 6.2.1618
= – –
living in 1630

Robert
bp 3.11 1619
died in infancy

Frances
bp 17.11.1619
= Henry Reston

Robert
bp 29.11.1620
bd 1.5.1626

George
bp 3.10.1622
bd 10.4.1623

John
bp7.4.1624
= Frances
Humphreys
6.11.1649
Pinchbeck.
Frances bd
2.4.1656

Robert
living 1630

John
bp 19.12.1654
= Frances – ?– c. 1670 aged 16/17
John's will 7.1.1679
Proved 30.8.1680.
John bd 24.7.1680.

William
bp 19.12.1654
bd 15.1.1655

Elizabeth
bp 13.10.1653
bd 18.2.1655

Thomas
bp 3.6.1652
No trace of
marriage
or issue

Mary
bp 30.8.1650

3. Children by Ann

Elizabeth

Audrey
bp –
bd 7.3.1650

John
bn c 1670
living on 7.1.1679
Succeeded his father
in July 1680.
bd 12.11.1680

Robert
bp 12.9.1672
no trace of
marriage or issue.
Living in 1680.

Ferdinand
bp 22.7.1674
bd 13.2.1697
No trace of
marriage or issue.

Male line dies out.

Key

b = Born
bp = Baptised
bd = Buried
c = circa (or about)
d = Died
= = Married
– – = Name not
known

* = previous page
and below

---

* The names of these seven children are not known. Nor are the baptismal dates of the other four known. However of ten baptisms in the Swineshead registers, where the parentage is not given, some almost certainly refer:

John 22.9.1586; Frances 28.3.1589; Thomas 20.8.1589; Edward 31.7.1592; Francis 18.7.1593; Alexander 27.12.1593; Jane 23.6.1594; Alice 10.9.1595; and Ann 20.5.1599.

William, the eldest son of Sir John Lockton and Dame Frances, was born about 1584. Little information is available for the remaining child Susanna, although there is an inventory relating to her dated 1615, where she is described as 'single woman'.

Another line of this manorial family in Swineshead had died out earlier in the century. This line came down from Philip Lockton, brother of John Lockton whose origins were in Cawston, Cambridge:

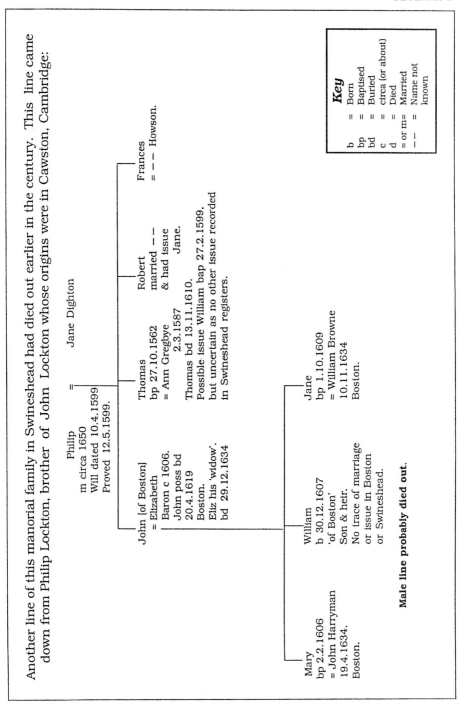

Philip
m circa 1650
Will dated 10.4.1599.
Proved 12.5.1599.

= Jane Dighton

Thomas
bp 27.10.1562
= Ann Gregbye
2.3.1587
Thomas bd 13.11.1610.
Possible issue William bap 27.2.1599.
but uncertain as no other issue recorded
in Swineshead registers.

Robert
married – –
& had issue
Jane.

Frances
= – – Howson.

John [of Boston]
= Elizabeth
Baron c 1606.
John poss bd
20.4.1619
Boston.
Eliz his 'widow'.
bd 29.12.1634

Jane
bp 1.10.1609
= William Browne
10.11.1634
Boston.

William
b 30.12.1607
'of Boston'
Son & heir.
No trace of marriage
or issue in Boston
or Swineshead.

Male line probably died out.

Mary
bp 2.2.1606
= John Harryman
19.4.1634.
Boston.

Key

b	=	Born
bp	=	Baptised
bd	=	Buried
c	=	circa (or about)
d	=	Died
= or m	=	Married
– –	=	Name not known

APPENDIX 2

THE PLAGUE OF 1636

William Lockton was a signatory to a document issued during the plague of 1636, giving: 'Orders to be observed by the Inhabitants of ye Wappentakes of Kirton, Skirbeck, and Elloe, dureinge the time of this Visitation.' It is a lengthy document and the following are only extracts.

'First, That all such persons as are visited and infected with the Plague, (being not able to live of themselves) bee speedily conveyed into some out parte of the Towne, where least recourse of people is used, And them of ability, to bee kept at their owne houses at their owne chardge, and a Collection to be gathred aswell for the releivinge of the said poore visited and infected.'

'Item that there bee (dureinge the time of their visitation) a sufficient & carefull watch kept over all those that shalbe infected, to restraine them from goeing abroad & keepinge company wth others yt bee sounde.'

'Item yf any dye in any part of the Towne where any doubt or suspicion may arise to be the plague, the body of that person not to be burryed untill it bee viewed, to the end that if it bee the plague Order may be taken to restraine the rest of the family from goeinge abroade, and a Crosse to bee sett upon the doore.'

'Item That noe person wch is knowne to dye of the plague shall bee burryed in the day time, but eyther in the morninge before sonnriseinge, or in the Eveninge after sunnsettinge when most people are in their houses, and at rest.'

'Item that all persons within the said Townes upon open warninge given in the church, shall keepe their Doggs, Catts, & Swyne surely chayned or tyed upp, or else hange them, that they goe not abroade especially in the night, and after warninge given if any dogge shal be takeb abroade out of his Maisters house, to be killed and burryed by some appoynted for that purpose, and they to have of the owner of such dogge, two pence.'

'Item that two substanciall men bee appoynted by the Minister, & foure, thre, or two of the cheife Inhabitants as aforesaide to Collecte and gather all such summes of monie as shall bee assessed of the Inhabitants for the maynteynance and releife of such poore persons as are visited and restrayned from going abroade.'

'Item that there bee some carefull woeman appoynted to keepe & looke too the poore & sick visited persons, and when any shall dye, they to wynde them, and bringe them out of the houses, that they may be viewed.'

'Item that the beddinge and other clothes worne or used by the diseased soe soon as all the partyes diseased bee recovered, or deade, bee either burnte, or ayred as is pr'scribed by the Phisicians set down in his Ma'ties Booke of Orders'

'Item Wee doe order that the Mercers in every Towne shall provide and have in readynesse London-treacle, and Methridate of the beste, and such other matterials for medecines as is sett forth in the booke printed by his Ma'tys Commande as a direction for this tyme of Visitation.'

'Item We doe Order yt ten pounds weekly shalbe levyed upon ye Towns of Swinshead, Wigtoft, Sutterton, Algakirk, & Fossdyke, Kirton, Frampton, Wiberton over Skirbek quarter & Broth'rtoft. And also out of & upon the Townes of Skirbeck, Fishtoft, Freeston, Leverton, Benington, Butterwick & Leake accordinge to the auncient rates that every Towne doth beare unto Comon Countrey chargs. Md these two last Orders were made at ye first Meetinge, ye xviijth of August.'

The signatories were: Edward Heron, J. Brooke, Anth: Irbye, W:. Lockton, Be: Wymberley, and Dymoke Walpole. 23 August 1636
[The document was issued by the signatories who were His Majesty's Commissioners locally.]

APPENDIX 3

[RE. CHAPTER THREE]

TAKEN FROM A BOARD IN ST. MARY'S CHURCH
RECTORS OF SWINESHEAD

Date of instn	Name	Patron
1201	JOHN "Parson of Swineshead" in 1201 Rector of a mediety of the Church of Swineshead	
1239/40	ADAM DE ASTON subdeacon	Mrgery Gresl
1248/9	ALEXANDER DE HOYLAND deacon Presented to Conisholme 1204 "to be held with the church of Swineshead". He was Official of the Archdeacon of Lincoln 1262/3.	Margery de Gredlee
1271	JOHN DE UPTON subdeacon, Leydet, on death of Alexander previously Rector of Caldicote, Hunts.	The Lady Christiana
1287	JOHN DE AULA clerk in minor orders	The Lady Hawisa de Grele
	JOHN DE LA SALE died about 1321	indulgence dated 1322 to pray for the soul of John de Aula rector of Swineshead buried in
1321	JOHN DE CLAIDEN acolyte	the chancel of Puriton, Som. John de la Warre, Knt.
1327	HENRY DE EDENSTOWE	" "
1331	JOHN DE SUTTON	" "
1340	ALEXANDER DE OUNESBY on death of John de Sutton	" "
1340/1	HENRY DE EDENSTOWE By exchange with Alexander for the church of Caistor, Lincs.	
1340/50	THOMAS DE WYK acolyte. on death of Henry	Joan wife of Sir John de la Warre.
1351	ALEXANDER GRELLE priest.	
1364	THOMAS WYKE OF ASSEWELL priest	Thomas de Wyke of Skerdington & John Wyke
	THOMAS DE RODESTON executor of the will of Roger de la Warre Knight 1368	
1378	THOMAS DE LA WARRE clerk He was lord of the manor of Manchester.	John la Warre kt
1382	JOHN DE MARCHFORD	" "
1386	JOHN PRESTWOLD priest	" "
1394	THOMAS LE WARRE priest	" "

1400	NICHOLAS MOTTE priest.	Thomas la Warre
		Lord de la Warre
1422	THOMAS LA WARRE clerk.	Thomas Bishop
		of Durham, Richard
	WILLIAM LOFT clerk	Lumbard & Richard
	died about 1466.	Frith, Thomas Sutton
1466	WILLIAM ROWSING Priest	& Thomas Rowsyng
1493	HUGH OLDHAM priest.	Margaret Countess
	He became Bishop of Exeter and was founder	of Richmond
	of Manchester Grammar School.	& Derby mother
	Buried Exeter Cath.	of King Henry

VICARS OF SWINESHEAD

1500	JOHN MARSHALL priest	The Abbot and Convent
		of Westminster
1504/5	JOHN MASON priest	" "
1508/9	THOMAS GARTON priest	" "
1537	THOMAS HAREBY clerk	" "
1551	ROBERT FORSTER clerk	Trinity College Cambridge
1554	THOMAS TOMSON clerk	" " "
1560	WILLIAM WILTON clerk.	The Bishop of
	Graduated Cambridge B.A.1536. Instituted to	Lincoln
	Rectory of Fleet 1562 where he resided.	
	He lost his letters of orders in the time of	
	Queen Mary when he was persecuted.	
1564	JOHN BILLINGSLEY clerk	Trinity College
	B.A. Camb 1562	Cambridge
	THOMAS DEANE clerk (compounded for firstfruits 1571)	
1576/7	WILLIAM BALDERSTONE ordained priest 1583	
	B.A. Trinity College Cambridge	
1592	ADAM ABRAHAM M.A.	Trinity College
	Vicar of Chard, Somerset 1603/36	
1599	WILLIAM HUDSON M.A.	Trinity College
		Cambridge
	RAPHAEL EDWARDS clerk.	
	Bishop's certificate of his admission 31 May 1615.	
1619	WILLIAM HARDWICKE, clerk	Trinity College
	"re-instituted 1621, on the presentation of the	Cambridge
	King to confirm his title" M.A. Trinity College	
	Cambridge. Vicar of Bicker 1631.	
1631	GEORGE BROWNINGE M.A. of Trinity College Cambridge	
1644	SAMUEL SOTHEBIE was appointed Parish Register in the	
	Commonwealth. Married. Buried at Swineshead.	
1675	JOHN JENNINGS clerk.	
	Buried beneath a marble slab in the nave of Swineshead.	

163.

	THOMAS MADOCKS clerk of Trinity College	
	no degree	
1715	FRANCIS GOUGH clerk.	
	B.A. of Trinity College Cambridge.	
1760	ROBERT UVEDALE clerk.	
	Fellow of Trinity D.D.1772. Rector of Langton 1764/99.	
1800	JAMES WILLIAM DODD clerk, son of James William Dodd,	
	the well known actor, of Bury, Suffolk.	
	Usher of Westminster School,1784. Buried in the	
	east cloister of Westminster Abbey where there is	
	a memorial to him.	
1811	WILLIAM BOLLAND clerk. His death was	
	occasioned by a fall from a carriage whilst watching	
	the illuminations in London for the Queen's marriage.	
1840	JOSEPH WATKINS BARNES clerk M.A.	
	of Trinity College.	
1844	HENRY LEE GUILLEBAND clerk. M.A.	
	Cambridge	
1848	JOSEPH HOLMES clerk. B.A.	
	Built the vicarage at Swineshead.	
1912	ROBERT EDWARD BARLOW POOLE clerk.	
	M.A. Keble College Oxford.	
1919	ARCHIBALD ORMSTON HAYES	The Bishop of
	M.A. of Merton College Oxford.	Lincoln
1923	CHRISTOPHER JAMES GURNHILL	" "
	B.A. of Emmanuel College Oxford.	
1938	JOHN GEORGE HAWLEY CRAGG	
	Chaplain to the Forces.	
1976	LESLIE GORDON STANDLEY M.A.,Dip.Th.	

NOTE:

Rector   A clergyman who had a right to the total revenues of the parish, i.e. tithes, rentals, etc.

Vicar   A clergyman who received only a part of the total revenues, usually the income from the glebe land, small tithes and the use of the vicarage. (This office arose after the suppression of the monasteries when parish revenue was invested in the crown and then transferred to beneficiaries such as colleges, cathedrals or lay individuals. The recipient of the total parish revenue would then agree the vicar's entitlement).

APPENDIX 4

DETAILS FROM THE ENCLOSURE DOCUMENTS
THE 1767 ACT:

Written on the outer cover:

A N
A C T
FOR

Dividing a certain Fen called the
Haute Huntre, Eight Hundred
Or Holland Fen and certain other
commonable Places adjoining
thereto, in the Parts of Holland
in the County of Lincoln

[1767]

Also on the outer cover is written:

"887 Houses in the 11 Towns pay Kings tax
63 - perhaps so many more that do not pay."

Inside, the document refers to Holland Fen and adjacent places "containing by Estimation Twenty-two Thousand Acres . . . wherein the Owners and Proprietors of Houses and Toftsteads within the Eleven Parishes, Townships or Places following: have Right of Common, and also within a certain place called Dogdyke in the Parish of Billinghay: and also there are several old inclosed Lands within the said Parishes . . . which have been always charged to the Dike-reeve Assessments for . . . the preservation of the said fen."

The Act provided for the appointment of Commissioners, the counting of houses and the survey and measurement of the affected land. The Commissioners were then authorised to sell and dispose of the "Rights of Average and Common" over Mown Rakes.

Zachary Chambers esq, Lord of the Manor of Swineshead and Charles Anderson Pelham, Lord of the Manor of Frampton, were "jointly entitled to the Soil of the said Fen" and Charles Pelham was also entitled "to the Brovage or Agistment of Four hundred and Eighty Head of Cattle . . . upon the said Fen yearly from old May Day to old Michaelmas."

The commissioners assigned unto Zachary Chambers and his heirs "One Plot or Parcel of Ground to contain One hundred and Twenty Acres of the said Fen . . . on the East side of the New River in a certain Part of the said Fen called Brand End."

They allotted to Charles Pelham "One Plot or Parcel of Ground to contain One hundred and Twenty Acres of the said Fen . . . laid out to adjoin . . . . the Place called the Great Beets," and also to Charles Pelham in compensation for his Right of Brovage "One other plot . . . . to lie contigious to the last mentioned Allottment, the same to consist of such and the like Number of Acres. (The number of acres not mentioned but the subject of an award made on 5th April 9 James I.)"

After these allotments to Chambers and Pelham, the residue of the land was to be let out and alloted to the eleven parishes and places in proportion to the number of houses having right of common. It was said that the Commissioners should "in the First Place let out and allot Four Acres for . . . every House or Tenement, and Two

Acres for . . . each Toftstead." These allotments were to be deemed common Fen belonging to each parish or township.

The 1773 Bill:

In 1773 a Bill was passed for dividing and enclosing land in Swineshead village and Wigtoft Marsh:

A
B I L L
FOR

Dividing and Inclosing the Several Parcels of Fen and other Common-able Lands within the Parish of Swineshead, in the County of Lincoln, and also a certain Plot of Land called Wigtoft Marsh, in and near to the said Parish of Swineshead.

[1773]

This Bill refers to the previous Act and reaffirms that Charles Anderson Pelham and Zachary Chambers "were Lords of Two Third Parts of the Soil of the said Fen, and were entitled to Two Third Parts of the Brovage thereof: for which Rights Compensation has been made to them respectively: And whereas the Right Honourable Brownlow Earl of Exeter, as Lord of the Soke of Kirton, is Lord of the Third remaining Part of the Soil of the said Fen, and is also entitled to the Third remaining Part of the Brovage thereof, for which no Compensation has yet been made . . . "

It goes on to provide for the allotment of Wigtoft Marsh and to confirm "in what Manner the Fen Land, alloted to Swineshead shall be disposed of."

167.

The Enclosure Award of 1774:

HOLLAND ENCLOSURE AWARD 36 [1774]

Firstly three commissioners were sworn in to officiate over the proceedings:

"To all to whom these Presents shall come We Peter Packharnis of Bruington in the county of Lincoln, Thomas Hogard of Spalding in the County aforesaid and William ffillingham of ffareborough in the County of Nottingham Gentlemen Commissioners appointed by an Act of Parliament made and passed in the thirteenth year of the Reign of his present Majesty intituled "An Act for dividing and enclosing the several parcels of ffen and other commonable Lands within the parish of Swineshead in the County of Lincoln and also a certain plot of Land called Wigtoft Marsh . . ."

Peter Packharnis, Thomas Hogard and William Fillingham took the following oath at The Griffin Inn on 19th July 1773:

"I Peter Packharnis [Thomas Hogard . . . William Fillingham . . .] do swear that I will faithfully and impartially and honestly according to the best of my Skill and Judgement hear and determine all such Matters and Things as shall be brought before me as a commissioner by virtue of an Act ffor dividing and enclosing the several parcels of ffen and other commonable Lands Within the parish of Swineshead in the County of Lincoln and also a certain plot of Land called Wigtoft Marsh in and near to the said parish of Swineshead without ffavour whatsoever so help me God."

The document goes on to designate land belonging to the various charities of Swineshead. Allotted to the poor of the village were 2 roods and 15 perches of land in the Rakes near "the Long Road lying East, the said William Stead's allotment West & South, and the said Wildbore Garner's allotment", and also 2 roods and 7 perches in Far Cattle Holme.

The allotments were:

Trustees of Fosters Charity - with Robert Wilby & William Hoyes (Fosters Charity had one rood 21 perches lying E & S Robert Wilby, the Old Eau West & the road or way North).

Trustees of Foster's Charity with   Trinity College.
" " "   " " Edward Moore.
" " "   " " William Stead esq.

Swineshead Poor with William Stead esq.
William Gee & Cecil Fairfax.

Sir Gilbert Heathcote	& Swineshead Poor.
Sir Gilbert Heathcote	& Thomas Stanser.
" " "	& Sir Sampson Gideon
" " "	& James Guznar.
" " "	& John Jessop Senior.
" " "	& Cowley's Charity.
" " "	& Robert Wilby.
" " "	& William Stead esq.
" " "	& Thomas Waite.
John Dickenson	& Sir Gilbert Heathcote
Sir Gilbert Heathcote	& Thomas Wright.
Thomas Wright	& Trustees of John Holland.
" "	& Trustees of Thomas Holland.
Trustees of John Holland	& Foster's Charity.
Wildbore Garner	& Eleanor Lister.
" " " "	& John Scudamore esq.
" " " "	& Sir Gilbert Heathcote.
" " " "	& William Stead esq.
" " " "	& James Harriman.
" " " "	& Trustees of Foster's Charity.
" " " "	& Swineshead Poor.
" " " "	& Robert Wilby.

William Gee & John Scudamore esq.

Individual allotments were made to:

Algarkirk cum Fosdyke Poor, Elizabeth Ayscough, Ashdales Feoffees, Thos Andis, Tho Ackland, John Allwood, Jane the wife of William Alvey, Bartholomew Barlow, Rev Edward Bayley, Rev

Richard Bailey, Boaz Baxter, Edward Baker, Roger Bates, William Bailey, Robert Barlow esq, Sarah Baxter, John Baxter, John Beale, Fra: Beaty, Peregrine Bertie esq, Rev Dr Beridge, Rev Basil Beridge, Bicker Parsonage, Robert Bingley, William Bird, Eliz Boulton, Sarah Bishop, Thomas Brittain, Ann Burt, Rev Robert Burne, Theo Buckworth esq, Dr Buckworth, James Burrell, Jonathan Brown, Thomas Burton, Butler's Trustees, Stephen Camwell, Thomas Carnell, Zacharias Chambers esq, Elizabeth Claypon, John Clifton, Robert Clifton, John Clarke, Richard Clay, Rev Dr Caryl Aquila Cash, John Chapman, James Cole, Cowley's & Blisbury's Charities, Sir George Smith, Samuel Crompton esq, Lady Cust, Robert Coleville esq, Margaret Crossby, John Cross, Samuel Crompton, Robert Collins, Thomas & Elizabeth Day, John Dickenson, Vicar of Deeping St James, Mrs C Davenport, Lady Dryden, Elizabeth Lawrence, Earl of Exeter, James Ellis, Rev George Fairfax, Rev Cecil Fairfax, Francis Fairfax, Catharine Fairfax, Earl Fitzwilliam, Thomas Fisher, Rev Richard Fox, Fosters Charity, John Fountain, Samuel Foster, Fosdyke Hospital, Samuel Forster, William Foster, Rev Wyatt Francis, John Frotheringham, Charles Gray, William Gee, Sir Sampson Gideon, William Golding, Hannah Granger, James Garnar, Wildbore Garnar, William Garfit, John Gainsborough, Thomas Harmstead, John Harness junior, Haceby Poor, Sir Gilbert Heathcote, William Hey, Katharine Hey, Joseph Heylin, James Hides, James Holbourn, Thomas Holland, John Holland, Elizabeth Hoyes, Thomas Houghton, William Hirst, John Hanley, William Hanley, Mary Hanley, John Harniss, John Jackson Harrison, Joseph Harrison, James Hardy, Joseph Hare, Samuel Hall, Sir Gilbert Heathcote, John Holland, the Rev Garvase Holmes, Horbling Poor, Robert Hutchinson, Ann Ingram, Thomas Ives, Curtis Jefferson, Thomas Jarvis, Mary Jarvis, William Jackson, John Jessop, Joshua Johnson, John King esq, Richard Lee, – Lenton, Eleanor Lister, Peter Lawrence, John Longthorne, Robert Leeson, Elizabeth Lillie, Sarah Lomax of Gunnerby, Elizabeth Lomax of Sleaford, Robert Longmate, Elizabeth Mason, Joseph Mason, Benjamin March, Henry Michael, Edward Moore, Ann Moore, Benjamin Muggliston, Henry Munk, John Michael Newton, Blisbury Pakey, John Pakey, Cowley Palmer esq, Benjamin Park, John Parrish, John Picker, Frances Preston, Elizabeth Preston, Charles Pilkington esq, Thomas Pike, David Pike, John Pike, John

Pine, Rev Lewin Powell, Francis Popham esq, Quakers Charity,
Samuel Reynardson esq, Judith Richards, William Ridley, Reuben
Risebrook, Michael Robinson, George Roberts, Thomas Sandon,
John Saul, John Scudamore esq, William Sleight, William Smith,
Richard Smith, Robert Smith, Spalding Poor, William Spendley,
Thomas Stanser, Jane Short, William Stead esq, Ann Stevens,
William Spurr, Squires heirs, Stanley's heirs, Sarah Smith,
Lawrence Stocks, Sutterton Poor, Swineshead Poor, George
Thornhill esq, William Taylor, William Faulkes, William Thacker,
Samuel Thompson, John Tunnard, Rev Brownlow Toller, Rev
Charles Trimnell, Hungerton & Vyral (Rectory), Richard Watson,
William Weekes, Wigtoft Poor, Thomas Wright, Lord Bishop of
Lincoln, Vicar of Wigtoft, James York Wilson, Ann Wilson, Thomas
Wright, Edward Wright, Alexander Wright, John Water, George
Wass, Thomas Waite, Thomas Wheldale, John Whitehead, John
White, Lord Willoughby de Broke, Robert Willoughby, Elizabeth
Wilby, John West, Eva Wadeson, Elizabeth Walton, William Watson
esq, Edward Watson, Robert Watson, Thomas York esq.

(dated) 19th July 1773. Griffin Inn, Swineshead.

APPENDIX 5 *[Re. Chapter Seven]*

THE WORKHOUSE
Swineshead parish register entries.

Baptisms

19.06.1814 John Taffock born June 14, 1814 son of Martha Ruddam, spinster, Swineshead Workhouse, Tarry Hill.

24.08.1815 John Pearson born Aug 23 1815 son of Elizabeth Auckland, spinster, Swineshead Workhouse, Tarry Hill.

01.12.1815 Harriet born Nov 30 1815, dtr of Hannah Spittlehouse, spinster, Workhouse, Tarry Hill in Swineshead.

26.04.1816 Mary born April 24th 1816 dtr of Elizabeth Woods spinster, Workhouse, Tarry Hill in Swineshead.

23.07.1816 Hopkin born July 20th 1816, son of Maria Pell, spinster, Workhouse, Tarry Hill in Swineshead.

29.08.1816 Hugh, born August 28th 1816, son of Ann White, spinster, Workhouse, Tarry Hill in Swineshead.

25.09.1816 Ann d of Elizabeth Lister, spinster, Workhouse, Tarry Hill, in Swineshead.

01.05.1817 Catherine dt of William & Sarah Tidswell, Bricklayer. Workhouse, Tarry Hill in Swineshead.

08.10.1817 William son of Sarah Lanes, spinster, Workhouse, Tarry Hill in Swineshead.

20.12.1817 Eleanor dtr of Elizabeth Williams, spinster, Workhouse, Tarry Hill in Swineshead.

16.01.1818 Rebecca dtr of Sarah Wilcock, spinster, Workhouse, Tarry Hill in Swineshead.

19.04.1818 Goodyear son of Martha Taylor, spinster, Workhouse, Tarry Hill in Swineshead.

23.06.1818 Charles son of Ann Thorlby, spinster, Workhouse, Tarry Hill in Swineshead.

29.12.1818 Richard Taylor son of Mary Stretton, spinster, Workhouse, Tarry Hill in Swineshead.

29.12.1818 Naomi Edwards dt Charlotte Cartwright, spinster, Workhouse, Tarry Hill in Swineshead.

02.04.1819 William son of John & Mary Chamberlain, labourer. Workhouse, Tarry Hill in Swineshead.

01.02.1821 Frederick son of John & Mary Chamberlain, labourer. Workhouse, Tarry Hill in Swineshead.

25.03.1821 James son of John & Mary Allam, labourer. Workhouse, Tarry Hill in Swineshead.

22.02.1824 Elizabeth dtr of Hannah Roberts, spinster, Workhouse, Tarry Hill in Swineshead.

25.03.1824 Holmes son of Rebecca Kew, spinster, Workhouse, Tarry Hill in Swineshead.

BURIALS

27.08.1815 John Pearson Auckland Infant   Swineshead Workhouse
01.08.1815 Ann Tall aged 76   "   "
08.09.1815 Richard Barnwell alias Fisher aged 63 "   "
20.01.1816 Harriet Spitalhouse Infant   "   "
09.05.1816 Mary Woods Infant   "   "
03.02.1817 Ann Lister Infant   "   "
26.08.1817 James Duffy, an Irishman age 26   "   "
02.01.1818 Eleanor Williams Infant   "   "
09.04.1818 Sarah Filer age 7   "   "
05.07.1818 James Barber Infant   "   "
16.03.1819 Mary Stretton age 25   "   "
21.08.1819 Barney Mackabe age 19   "   "
13.09.1819 John William Kealey age 53   "   "
22.12.1819 Thomas Waters age 23   "   "
14.02.1821 Frederick Chamberlain Infant   "   "
25.02.1821 Mary Chamberlain age 26   "   "

NB: Several burials in 1796/7 are noted as 'smallpox'. In 1798 ten infants died with measles and one by 'Verdict By Visitation of God'.

Appendix 6   *[Re. Chapter Ten]*

Public Houses

In the 1930s Swineshead still had fourteen public houses in the village and surrounding area. These included the Royal Oak and the Elephant & Castle in South Street, both now private houses; The Green Dragon and The Wheatsheaf, both still operating in the Market Place; The Red Lion in High Street, now an art shop; and the Griffin which stood at the corner of Church Lane.

In the direction of the station was The Black Swan on the left hand side of the road just before Tarry Hill; the Golden Cross at North End, still a public house today; The King's Head and the New Inn both at North End but no longer there; and The Plough and The Barge which are both still in business. In the other direction, at Fenhouses, was a public house called The Ball, and at Baythorpe, on the corner of the junction with the old main road was The Lion, now a private house.

The following is a list of the various landlords of Swineshead public houses, but may be incomplete. The main sources of reference for these were the census and local directories up to 1933.

Elephant & Castle - South Street

1896   William Faulkner (who was also a farmer)
1913   Robert Francis Horn
1933   Harry Booth

Royal Oak - South Street

1933   John Richard Pordham

THE WHEATSHEAF - Market Place

1820	Some time after 1820, Edward Cole, landlord of the Neptune Inn on the river bank near Skirbeck church, moved to Swineshead to become the landlord of the Wheatsheaf.
1826	William Kirkham
1841	John Jessop
1849	John Jessop (also brewer)
1856	Seth Cawthorne
1861	Seth Cawthorne
1876	James Ward
1891	John Pickersgill
1896	Joseph Whitworth (also potato merchant and receiver of the mail)
1913	Ernest Callow Stammers
1927	Robert Wilkinson Kealey
1933	Henry George Morriss

GREEN DRAGON - Market Place

1826	George Cook
1841	Christopher Howard
1849	John Elliott
1856	Richard Fox
1861	Dickenson Lynne
1876	Dickenson Lynne
1881	Dickenson Lynne
1891	Dickenson Lynne
1896	Albert Sparrow
1913	Mrs Isabella Evans
1933	William Frederick Trevor

THE BLACK BULL - Market Place

1826	William Fox
1851	possibly John Gunson
1856	Maria Bonner
1861	Maria Bonner
1876	William Hall
1891	Samuel Middlebrooke
1896	Samuel Middlebrooke

GRIFFIN INN - High Street/Church Lane

1826	James Sumpter
1841	Henry Smith
1849	Henry Smith
1856	Robert Simpson Carlisle (who was also the church organist)
1861	John Brown Jessop
1876	John Brown Jessop
1881	George Tomlinson and Mary his wife
1891	Ellen Gamble
1896	Daniel Burton Waldegrave
1913	Joseph Brown Wilson
1933	Mrs Florence Smart

RED LION - High Street (once known as Church Street)

1826	John Thornton
1841	Robert Lupton
1849	Sarah Dewhurst
1851	William Marshall
1856	John Sharp
1861	John Pickering
1876	Richard Maddison
1881	Richard Maddison and his wife Ann
1896	Charles Hardy
1913	Mary Jane Hardy
1933	Mary Hardy

SWAN INN - Tarry Hill

1826	Catharine Warsop
1841	George Monks
1849	George Monks
1851	Mary Monks (widow)
1856	Phoebe Martin
1861	William Burden
1876	Richard Brown
1881	Richard Brown and Jemima his wife.
1896	(not stated whether Tarry Hill or High Street) James Middlebrooke
1913	(not stated whether Tarry Hill or High Street) James Middlebrooke

176.

BLACK SWAN - High Street

1933   Mrs Charlotte Middlebrooke

GOLDEN CROSS - North End

1826   Isaac Thornton
1841   Mark Hodson
1849   Edward Housely
1856   William Horby
1861   William Rawlinson
1876   George William Rawlinson
1881   George Rawlinson
1891   Mrs Rachel Rawlinson
1896   Mrs Rachel Rawlinson
1913   Mrs Rachel Rawlinson
1933   George Alfred Pordham

NEW INN - North End

1933   George Bell (beer retailer)

KING'S HEAD - North End

1826   Edward Watson
1841   Michael Peart
1849   Bradley Pierce
1856   John Baines
1861   Jacob Hardy
1876   George Espin
1933   Victor Rawlinson

THE PLOUGH - Sleaford Road, Swineshead Bridge

1876   Cornelius Dalton (given as a beer retailer in White's Directory)
1881   Cornelius Dalton, and his wife Emma
1891   Frederick William Green (also a wheelwright)
1896   Frederick William Green
1933   Jesse Andrew (described as a beer retailer)

The Barge - Swineshead Bridge

1826   William Barnes
1841   John Sewell
1849   William Drury
1856   William Drury
1861   Thomas Burden
1876   William Butler
1881   William Butler (the Barge then known as The Railway Hotel).
1896   William Butler
1913   Richard Anthony Greetham (Barge still known as The Railway Hotel).
1933   Harry Morton Oliver (Still The Railway Hotel).

Golden Ball - Fenhouses

1826   Samuel Holland
1841   John Brackenbury
1849   James Brackenbury
1851   James Brackenbury
1856   James Brackenbury
1876   William Thorpe
1896   Richard Craft
1933   Thomas Robinson or John Pickwell

The Lion - Baythorpe

1933   Derek Nundy (beer retailer)

1849 Beer sellers: John Allbones; Charles Clements, North End; Thomas Favell; William Herd; John Skinner, Gibbet Hills; William Tyler, Drayton; John Walker, North End.

1896 Beer retailers: Robert Buffham; Stephen Lucas; William Lunn, (who was also a blacksmith); and Mrs Rachel Stevenson.
Isaac Bentley was a brewer's agent; and Mrs Mary Greetham was the agent for W & A Gilbey Ltd, Wine & Spirit Merchants.

1913 Beer retailers: Robert Buffham; Mrs Tamar Lunn; James Nundy; John Richard Pordham; Thomas Woods; Isaac Bentley - brewer's agent.

A MYSTERY PICTURE
?

180.

48. A group photograph outside The Green Dragon. Can you help?

This picture of forty-one men and two boys has, at the moment, no caption to accompany it as, so far, no one has been able to identify it. Can you help?

It was obviously taken outside 'The Green Dragon' hotel in the Market Place and the photographer's authentification is shown just below the actual photograph. 'Bliss' and (? of) Grantham appear to be the names but, although 'Bliss' is plain enough 'Grantham' could possible be open to other interpretations.

Samuel Evans is not listed as a licensee but it seems quite possible that Mrs Isabella Evans was his widow continuing with the licence perhaps after his death. As Albert Sparrow was the licensee in 1896 and Mrs Evans the licensee in 1913 the timing of the group portrait as being in the first decade of this century would be in keeping with the clothes and formal posing of the group.

Who are they? What group of men would have just two boys included? Were the boys there perhaps merely by chance or because they were the landlord's sons?

There are other possible clues in the group (they do, for example, all appear to be in their 'Sunday best' with highly polished shoes) but the author would be grateful for any additional identification. Perhaps— indeed quite likely— someone in the village has a photograph of one or two of the men in a family picture hanging on the wall or in an album. If you can help, the author would be glad to hear from you. If you do not know her present address any letter sent to the publisher will be forwarded.

REFERENCES

Books

Albert, William. *The Turnpike Road System in England 1663-1840.* (1972).

Ancliffe, V. *Two Moated Sites in South Lincolnshire* South Lincolnshire Archaeology: 4 (1980).

Anderson, C. L. *Lincolnshire Convicts to Australia, Bermuda and Gibraltar*

Andrews, C. Bruyn. *Torrington Diaries. The tours through England and Wales of the Hon John Byng the late 5th Viscount Torrington between the years of 1781 and 1794.* Volume 2.

Bagley, George. *Boston: Its Story and People.* (1986).

Beastall, T W. *Agricultural Revolution in Lincolnshire.*

Brears, Charles. *Lincolnshire in the 17th and 18th Centuries.* (1940).

Brown, Cornelius. *Annals of Newark on Trent.* (1879).

Caplan, Maurice. *Life in the Shadow of the Workhouse.*

Cassell's Gazeteer of Great Britain & Ireland. Vols 5-6 (1897).

Chamber's Encyclopaedia.

Cox, J. Charles. *Lincolnshire* (1916).

Curtis & Boultwood. *An Introductory History of English Education since 1800* (1960).

Darby, H. C. *Medieval Fenland.* (1940)

Dugdale, William. *Monasticon Anglicanum* Vol V.

English Place Name Society. *Place Names of Lincolnshire* (1985).

Eden, F. M. *State of the Poor II.*

Gibbons. *Notes on the Visitation of Lincolnshire 1634.*

Gosden, P. H. J. H. *The Friendly Societies in England 1815-1875.*

Hallam, H. E. *Settlement and Society. A Study of the Early Agrarian History of South Lincolnshire.*

Hammond, J. L. & B. *The Village Labourer 1760-1832.* (1911).

Hindley, Geoffrey. *A History of Roads* (1971).

Hissey, James John. *Over Fen and Wold.* (1898).

Horn, Pamela. *Labouring Life in the Victorian Countryside.* (1976).

Humble, Richard. *The Fall of Saxon England.*

Knowles, Dom David. *The Monastic Order in England from the times of St. Dunstan to the Fourth Lateran Council 940-1216.* (1963).

Lincolnshire Notes and Queries Vol 23.

Lincolnshire Pedigrees Vol III.

Lincs Record Society Vol 22. *Lincs Assize Rolls 1202-1209*

Lincs Record Society Vol 78. *The 1341 Royal Inquest in Lincolnshire.*

Lloyd, L. C. and Stenton, D. M. *Sir Christopher Hatton's Book of Seals.*(1950).

Marrat, W. *Sketches Historical & Descriptive in the County of Lincolnshire* (1813).

Morton, H. V. *In Search of England.* (1927).

Mee, Arthur. *Lincolnshire.* (1949).

Mee, Arthur. *The King's England.*

Murray's *Handbook of Lincolnshire* (1903).

Owen, Dorothy M. *Church and Society in Medieval Lincolnshire.* Volume V History of Lincolnshire Series.

Padley, J. S. *Fens and Floods of Mid-Lincolnshire* (1882).

Poole, A. L. *From Domesday Book to Magna Carta 1087-1216* Oxford History of England Series.

Ravensdale, J. R. *History on your doorstep.*

Richards, Julian D. *Viking Age England* (1991).

Savage, Anne (trans by) *Anglo-Saxon Chronicles* (1982).

Southworth, John, *The English Medieval Minstrel.* (1989).

Streatfield, G. S. *Lincolnshire and the Danes.* (1884)

Stukeley, *Itinerarium Curiosum* (1724).

Thirsk, Joan. *English Peasant Farming: the Agrarian History of Lincolnshire from Tudor to Recent Times.* (1957).

Thompson, Pishey. *The History and Antiquities of Boston* (1856).

Venables, E. *Chronicon Abbatiae de Parco Lude 1066-1413.* (1891).

Victoria History of the County of Lincolnshire. Vol II.

Wailes, Rex. *Lincolnshire Windmills* Parts I & II. Post Mills & Tower Mills.

Webb, Sidney and Beatrice. *English Local Government; English*

Poor Law History Part I. The Old Poor Law. (1927).

Wheeler, W. H. *A History of the Fens of South Lincolnshire* (1896).

Whitaker's *Peerage, Baronetage, Knightage and Companionage* 1915.

White, W. *Eastern England* (1865).

Wilkinson, G. J. *Illustrated Lincolnshire* (1900).

Wright, Neil. *Lincolnshire Towns and Industry 1700-1914.* History of Lincolnshire Vol XI.

Other sources.

Unpublished material: Brian Simmons MA, FSA, MIFA.

Swineshead: A Short History of The Parish; The Parish Church of St Mary the Virgin; The Free Chapel of St Adrian within the Manor of Swineshead; The Cistercian Abbey of St Mary the Virgin. Rev J. G. H. Cragg, Vicar of Swineshead.

Swineshead Parish Coronation Souvenir Programme - *Our Ancient Heritage* Rev J. G. H. Cragg. (1977).

Pamphlet entitled *Restoration of St Mary's Church, Swineshead, Lincolnshire1868-1869.*

Pamphlet entitled: *An Act for Confirming a Scheme as amended of the Charity Commissioners for Cowley's Charity in the Parish of Swineshead in the County of Lincoln 1858.*

Swineshead Silver Band Centenary Souvenir Booklet.

Fenland Notes & Queries Vol 1, p 9 and Vol 3, pp 25-28, 76-78, 223-224.

Lincolnshire Notes & Queries Vol 23, pp 108-113.

Lincolnshire in 1719 (An old directory found at LAO)

Green's Lincolnshire Villages— Boston Library. Microfiche 4/3/ 177; 4/4/178-186.

Boston Guardian, Stamford Mercury and Boston Standard.

Lincolnshire Life— various.

Ross Manuscript at Lincoln Library.

White's Directories.

Kelly's Directories.

Hagar's Directory.

Interviews with local residents.

Documents at Lincolnshire Archives:

Wills at LAO:
John Lockton. Wills 1680/259.
Elizabeth Lockton. Wills 1647-8/406.
Inventory LAO:
Inv 1615; 265. Susan Lockton single woman.
Inv 154; 236. Eliz Lockton. 1647/8.
Notes taken in the church at Swineshead by Monson in 1833. Ref
LAO MONSON 27/1/2.
MISC DEP 259/4/1/7 John Brewster 1727.
Holland Quarter Sessions:
HQS/A/3/5-19
HQS/A/2/20
HQS/A/2/21
HQS/A/2/22
HQS/A/3/13.
Holland enclosure Award 36. 1774.
A Bill for Enclosing Swineshead Common: H77/1 & 2 [1773]
An Act for Enclosing Holland Fen: 1767. Holywell Papers Vol 2.
A Bill for Enclosing Swineshead Common: H77/1&2 [1773]
Sutton's Lincoln Roll
Boston Union Workhouse Admission & Discharge Book: PL1/3021
Licence for schoolmasters: Subs Book VIII/37 Subs Book VIII/95.
Census 1851/1881/1891.
Parish Registers and Bishop's Transcripts.

INDEX

A

B

190.

M